GODS OF MANAGEMENT

GODS OF MANAGEMENT

The Changing Work
of Organizations

CHARLES HANDY

OXFORD UNIVERSITY PRESS
New York   Oxford

Oxford University Press

Oxford   New York
Athens   Auckland   Bangkok   Bombay
Calcutta   Cape Town   Dar es Salaam   Delhi
Florence   Hong Kong   Istanbul   Karachi
Kuala Lumpur   Madras   Madrid   Melbourne
Mexico City   Nairobi   Paris   Singapore
Taipei   Tokyo   Toronto

and associated companies in
Berlin   Ibadan

First published in 1978 by Souvenir Press Ltd
Second edition 1985
Third edition 1991 by Business Books Ltd, an imprint of
Random House UK Ltd, reprinted under Century Business imprint 1992

Published by Oxford University Press, Inc., 1995

First issued as an Oxford University Press paperback, 1996

Oxford is a registered trademark of Oxford University Press

Library of Congress Cataloging-in-Publication Data
Handy, Charles B.
Gods of management: the changing work of organizations /
Charles Handy.
p.   cm.
Includes bibliographical references and index.
ISBN 0-19-509616-9
ISBN 0-19-509617-7 (Pbk.)
1. Management.   2. Organizational change—Management.
3. Corporate culture.   I. Title.
HD31.H3126   1995
658—dc20   94-39967

1 3 5 7 9 10 8 6 4 2

Printed in the United States of America

PREFACE

"Plus ça change, plus c'est la même chose," say the French, meaning that in life, it's often only the packaging that changes, that the truth beneath remains the same.

I feel this way about this book. I wrote the original edition in 1978, and it is still the book of which I am most proud. It has been updated and revised twice since then, and now a third time for this first American edition. Each time it has been necessary to change some of the numbers to bring them up-to-date and to add some more recent examples, but the underlying messages have remained constant over the years. These messages are

- There is no one right way to manage anything. Just as there are horses for courses and courses for horses, so there are ways that suit one situation and one type of business that are totally unsuited for another. Rather grandiosely I call this a theory of cultural propriety. If you can find the right culture or style for your situation, you will thrive, and if not, you will struggle.

- Cultures or styles can be classified. Building on an idea of Dr. Roger Harrison, who first identified the four types of organization that I use, I found four Greek gods who typified these cultures. This was not a device to amuse or to bemuse. The ancient Greeks had a wide choice of gods to worship, and they chose their favorite according to what he or she stood for. Individuals as well as organizations, I realized, had their natural and preferred cultures. Each was valid in its place, so the trick was to match the preferred gods of individual, organization, and situation.

• Time and technology have changed none of this thinking. Rather, what they have changed is the nature of work, the values of many of the people, and therefore the gods they now follow. Although the gods and the management cultures that they represent have not changed, the mix has, and this means a slow revolution in the way we run our organizations. In particular, Apollo, the god of order, precision, and, if you like, bureaucratic order, has lost his pole position. Athena, the warrior goddess and the patron of project groups and task forces, has come into her own, as have the Dionysians, the independents, and the free spirits among us.

• To succeed in the new world that is increasingly forcing itself on us, we must change our gods, and that is never easy. Old preferences stick, and old habits do not go away because logic says they should. Thus to change from Apollonian ways to Athenian requires a cultural revolution of sorts, and I shall try to describe what this means and how it might happen.

• If there are no right ways, there can be no sure guide to success. But this is not a "how to" book so much as an "aha" book, as when one says, "Aha, of course." Increasing our understanding of what is going on and why it is that way is all that I have ever tried to do.

It has long been my great sadness that although this book has been translated into many languages around the world, it has never before appeared in America. Perhaps it was too British, although most of the examples are drawn from America. Perhaps people thought, from the title, that it was a religious book or that I was making management into a religion, whereas, in truth, the gods of ancient Greece are the most pragmatic and earthy of gods.

This was sad for personal reasons. I first came to study management in America and have an enduring affection for the place. But it is sad, more seriously, because America seems the best placed of all countries to be able to cope with this changing mix of gods. They, of all peoples, should understand what the book is trying to accomplish. The decision, therefore, of Oxford University Press to publish this book for American readers gives me great pleasure. It is my rather presumptuous hope that this introduction to four gods of ancient Greece may shed some light on modern America.

Reading the book again in preparation for this edition, I realized, somewhat to my embarrassment, that everything that I have written about subsequently, particularly in *The Age of Unreason* and *The Age of Paradox* (both published by Harvard Business School Press), were foreshadowed somewhere in this book. I was reminded of the saying that every author writes only one book in his or her life, that every subsequent book is only a variation on that first theme. If that be so, then this is that book.

London   C.H.
October 1994

ACKNOWLEDGMENTS

To all those who contributed to my thinking, I am deeply grateful. If I have not acknowledged them in the text, it means only that they have entered my thought processes in some subliminal fashion. I live by the constant interchange of thought and ideas in teaching, argument, private discussion, or exchange of letters. I am grateful to all those colleagues, students, and friends who have, often unwittingly, contributed to my thinking.

Few, if any, of my ideas can be original. The notion of using Greek gods to symbolize cultures has been around for some time. Nietzsche used it, and so did Ruth Benedict. I was first introduced to it by Roger Harrison one sunny morning in the hills of Maine. I am grateful to him for this and many other ideas.

I first developed this idea in a chapter in *Understanding Organisations* (Penguin, 1985), in which I also present the theoretical underpinnings of the idea.

I am particularly grateful to Terry Hamaton, who has enlivened the text with his perceptive illustrations, and to my publishers for their constant stimulus and encouragement.

CONTENTS

GODS OF MANAGEMENT

Introduction

The gods in this book are the gods of ancient Greece. What, the reader may very understandably ask, do the gods of ancient Greece have to do with management? An explanation is needed.

To the Greeks, religion was more a matter of custom than a formal theology. Their gods stood for certain things, and to a degree, you chose your god because you shared the values and interests that they represented. You were a Zeus person or an Apollo person (the god of order and reason), a follower of Athena (the warrior goddess), or of Dionysus, to me the most individualist of the gods.

I have used these four gods to symbolize the different ways of managing that can be discerned in organizations or, to put it another way, the differing *cultures* that exist in organizations. I have done this not just to add whimsy to another book on management but to underline a very important point, that the management of organizations is not a precise science but more of a creative and political process, owing much to the prevailing culture and tradition in that place at that time. Organizations, like tribes and families, have their own ways of doing things, things that do work for them and things that don't work. You have to read them right to be effective.

To be sure, there are technical aids to management, principally ways of organizing and ordering numbers and materials; there are also some truths about the behavior of people and groups that seem to hold good in most situations. Wise managers make use of these aids and truths, but in themselves they are not enough; otherwise every student from a management course would be an expert manager. Management is more fun, more creative, more personal, more political, and more intuitive than any textbook. Nevertheless, even though every organization may be different, there are some patterns that can be discerned, models that can be imitated, and some guidelines that can be followed.

The patterns and models are those symbolized by the gods, representing different organizational cultures. They add up to what could be called a *theory of cultural propriety*, which holds that what matters is getting the right culture in the right place for the right purpose. It is a *low-definition* theory, one that suggests rather than prescribes and that is loose enough to allow room for the intuitive and the creative interpretation. No manager wants to be an automaton, nor should any organization be just a giant processing plant. It is the special privilege of being human that we can go beyond the theories and make our own rules. Organizations will never, therefore, be subject to precise laws and rigid theories. We should, as humans, be thankful for that, even if we might, as managers, occasionally wish it to be otherwise.

Part I of this book (Chapters 1 through 4) explains the theory of the cultures and how it applies to organizations. Most of the evidence to support the theory comes from personal experience, because unless concepts match one's own experience, creating that aha effect ("Aha! So that's why it happens like that!"), the theory will not be of practical use. I have laced the text, by way of anecdote, with bits of my own and other people's experiences, but the evidence that counts will come from the reader himself or, increasingly these days, herself. If each reader can identify Zeus figures, Apollonian structures, and Dionysian attitudes in their own surroundings, then the theory will begin to have a reality and a validity.

At one level, the theory helps explain the comfort or discomfort of an individual in an organization. That is, a follower of

Zeus will not be happy, or effective, in an Apollonian organization. An Apollonian manager will find Dionysians irritating beyond belief. At a second level, however, the theory becomes a diagnostic tool for a manager or consultant. Inappropriate cultures lead to unhappiness and inefficiency. Communication breakdowns are often the result of one culture clashing with another. Organizations nearly always need a mix of cultures to carry out their different tasks, but each culture must understand and respect the ways of the others. Too many organizations allow one culture to dominate and thus to impede the others.

Each culture, it will become clear, or each god, works on quite different assumptions about the basis of power and influence, what motivates people, how they think and learn, and how things can be changed. These assumptions result in quite different styles of management, structures, procedures, and reward systems. Each works well in certain situations, but get the wrong god in the wrong place and there will be trouble. The best way to run an efficient chocolate factory is not the right way to run an architects' partnership, an elementary school, or a construction site. Different cultures, and gods, are needed for different tasks. Cultures, too, need to change over time, as the tasks change, as the organization grows, or as people change. Much of the trouble in organizations comes from the attempt to go on doing things as they used to be done, from a reluctance to change the culture when it needs to be changed. The gods of management, after all, do arouse strong allegiances in their followers. Those who think like Zeus find it hard to accept that Apollo can ever be right.

Cultural confusion, therefore, is one of the principal ills that plague organizations. It shows up in inefficiency or, more obviously, in *slack,* the extra resources, the longer delivery times, the increased overtime, the overstaffed head office; slack is the organizational balm used to ease the pain of inefficiency. It is management's easy option and a way of cushioning a wrong culture. It is, however, expensive and can, in the end, kill the organization. Managers, therefore, need to be more aware of their own cultural predilections, of which god they personally follow, and more aware of the cultural choices that are open to them and to their organization. It was always a myth that there is one best way to manage, but it has been a pervasive myth and a damaging one, to both individuals and organizations. The Greeks at least recognized a variety of gods, even if each had his or her favorite. We need a law of requisite variety in management as well as a theory of cultural propriety.

Chapter 4 demonstrates that the choice of gods is influenced by their setting, by both the society around them and its national culture, and by the occupational setting of the organization. The Japanese are more fond of Apollo than are the Americans. Mexicans have a different way of working from the Swedes. Organizations must take account of these national differences. But a school has traditions different from those of a factory, and so does a hospital, and a nonprofit organization, or a church, is different again. The choice of organizational culture must take account of these differences as well. There is, I am glad to say, no one best way to manage.

Part II (Chapters 5 through 8) looks at the major cultural crisis affecting our organizations today. Briefly, it is that the chosen route to efficiency via concentration and specialization that resulted in the multilayered and multistructured organization and in an Apollonian or bureaucratic culture has reached a dead end. Scale creates costs as well as economies; it increases scope but can restrict flexibility; and more important, it runs counter to the cultural preferences of most of the people it needs to make it work. In sum, an Apollonian structure staffed by Athenians and Dionysians will be an expensive disaster.

Chapters 5 and 6 explain why this is so and why the chosen responses of most organizations will not work because they all seek to find ways of perpetuating the Apollonian dominance.

The answer lies in changing the balance of the gods. It adds up to a gradual *organization revolution,* which may come to be as important as the one that accompanied the industrial revolution. That revolution took people out of the villages into the towns, separated the workplace from the home, and transformed communities, family life, and the role of women. Whereas people used to work in gangs, they now worked in lines of anonymous "hands." The "factory" or the "office" became the daytime, or sometimes nighttime, house for most adults, a place where sometimes twenty thousand or more worked on one site, often for all their lives. The industrial revolution made the employment organization the linchpin of society, the means by which most people obtained not only their livelihood but also their status and their main purpose in life.

We have come to take the employment society for granted, although Marx and many others saw it as exploitative, alienating, and eventually doomed. So pervasive has it been that the right to work has come to mean the right to be employed, and it was confirmed as that in the Universal Declaration of Human Rights after World War II. The job may not have lived up to everyone's expectations, but a job was every man's right, and every woman's, too, if she wanted one.

If the employment organization, centered on the factory or the office, gives way, as Chapters 7 and 8 suggest it will, to a more contractual, dispersed, and federal organization, the effects on society will be profound. It will lead, on the one hand, to more small businesses, particularly in the services, and more self-employment. There will be more part-time work in all institutions and therefore more opportunities for more people to combine jobs with other interests in life. More work will be located near where people live rather than where the organization chooses to site itself. Communities could perhaps become more complete as more people live and work there rather than just sleep there. Flexilives and portfolios of work might become the norm rather than the exception.

On the other hand, the organization revolution could produce two classes of citizen once again: not, this time, the owners and the laborers, or the managers and the workers, but now those with careers and those with just jobs—the professionals and the hired help, who could easily be unhired. There would then be two labor markets, the primary market catering to the professionals and key staff, with job security and fringe benefits, and the secondary fringe of temporary labor, part-time help, and self-employed—free, maybe, but often poor.

If more self-employment and tiny businesses are one likely outcome of the organizational revolution then, in terms of the gods, we shall see a resurgence of Zeus and Dionysus, of individualism and personal power. For some countries, this might be more in tune with the national cultures than with the bureaucratic traditions of Apollo, but if these new forms of work are to be more than an impoverished fringe, there will have to be more thought given to how they can best cooperate and collaborate for their own success. Associations, agents, cooperatives, and partnerships belong to these cultures. Will they be the new emerging organizational forms? Can the new businesses learn from the nonprofit world and charitable organizations, in which the cultures of Zeus and Dionysus thrive, or from professional partnerships, schools, colleges, and the arts? Will society's older institutions turn out to be the models for the new ones?

Last but not least, our societies must adapt to the needs of the new breeds of organization. What kind of company law will be appropriate? Will stakeholders' rights still predominate, or will there have to be more recognition of the other stakeholders? What education is appropriate for a society of minientrepreneurs and semiprofessionals? How should taxation, pension, and social welfare policies be revamped for a world in which full-time employment for life will no longer be the norm? There are more questions than answers in this section, but they are included to demonstrate how an organization revolution inevitably extends its tentacles into every part of society. The gods of management must be taken seriously when they stage a palace revolution.

This book is thus an inquiry into the state of our organizations and their likely future. It is not intended to be a textbook or a manual for managers, although managers in all sorts of organizations should find it useful. It is written to encourage more people to think about how organizations actually work and what changes are on the way, because although 90 percent of those of us who work still do so in or for an organization, we still take their ways for granted as if they were part of nature's laws, to be marveled at or grumbled about but not by mere humans to be altered. If this book helps demystify organizations, makes their ways and their assumptions more understandable to ordinary mortals, and causes more people to think about the way in which they work and the ways in which they might have to work, it will have served its purpose.

The manager in this book is almost always referred to as *he*. This is not a deliberate attempt to ignore or demote the female half of the human race but is done to make the book easier to read. The male gods still predominate in organizations, so please take *he* to mean *he or she*. As the final chapter indicates, times are changing fast, and we may soon be using *she* as the predominant pronoun in management. That will indeed be a sign of an organizational revolution.

I

THE THEORY OF
CULTURAL PROPRIETY

1

The Four Gods
of Management

Each of the four gods gives its name to a cult or philosophy of management and to an organizational culture. Each of these cultures also has a formal, more technical, name, as well as a symbol, or picture. The name, picture, and the Greek god each

The Culture	The Picture	The God
Club		Zeus
Role		Apollo
Task		Athena
Existential		Dionysus

carries its own overtones, which combine to build up the concept I am trying to convey. They also help keep the ideas in one's memory. These names, signs, and gods do not amount to definitions, however, for the cultures cannot be precisely defined, only recognized when you see them. If you know anything about organizations, you should be able to recognize the descriptions as you read on.

It is important to realize that each of the cultures, or ways of running things, is *good*—for something. No culture, or mix of cultures, is bad or wrong in itself, only inappropriate to its circumstances. The fact that you do not like or approve of one of them makes it unsuitable for you, but not wrong or bad or inefficient in itself. This principle is the heart of the theory of cultural propriety, and I shall return to it again and again.

The Club Culture (Zeus)

The symbol for Zeus is a spider's web. The organization that uses this culture probably has, as all other organizations do, divisions of work based on functions or products. These are the lines radiating out from the center, like the lines of a traditional organization chart. But in this culture, these are not the lines that matter. Rather, the crucial lines here are the encircling ones, the ones that surround the spider in the middle, for these are the lines of power and influence, losing importance as they go farther from the center. The relationship with the spider matters more in this culture than does any formal title or position description.

Zeus is the patron god. The Greeks chose, or created, their gods to represent certain features of the world as they saw it. Zeus was the king of their gods, and he reigned on Mount Olympus by means of thunderbolts (when crossed) or showers of gold (when seducing). He was feared, respected, and occasionally loved. He represented the patriarchal tradition with his irrational but often benevolent power, impulsiveness, and charisma.

Historically, the club culture is found most frequently in the small entrepreneurial organization. The boat fanatic who finds he can sell the boats he builds, gets his son to help with manufacturing, his nephew to sell them, and his cousin to keep the accounts is Zeus, and that is the way Zeus slowly builds his web. But this culture also prevails in broking firms, in investment banks, in many political groupings, in start-up situations of all sorts, and on the bridge of many ships.

The club culture is an excellent one for *speed of decision.* Any situation to which speed is vital benefits from this style of management. Of course, speed does not guarantee quality. Rather, quality depends on the caliber of Zeus and of his inner circle: An incompetent, aging, or disinterested Zeus will quickly contaminate and slowly destroy his own web. *Selection* and *succession* are therefore rightly regarded as critical variables in these organizations, and much time and effort should be spent on them.

This culture achieves speed through an unusual form of communication—empathy. One afternoon I watched the young executive of a small broking firm at work in the precious metals exchange. He was making a series of rapid purchase and sale decisions, of what seemed to me to be alarming magnitudes, with no calculators, formulas, or resources to higher authority or expertise. "How do you make these decisions," I asked, "and what formal approval and authority do you need from your firm?" "Oh," he said, "I make my own decisions, but I try always to double-guess what the old man would do." "And if you fail?" I asked. "Curtains," he said, "for me."

The club culture can be cruel if your empathetic guess is wrong. But empathy needs no memos, committees, or formal authorities. Club cultures, indeed, are very short on documentation. Zeus does not write; he speaks, eyeball to eyeball, if possible, if not, then by telephone. Many a successful Zeus has been illiterate, if not always innumerate. Instead, empathy depends on *affinity* and *trust.*

You cannot guess what the other man is thinking unless you think like him. There is little empathy between opposites. Your brother's son, your tennis partner, or your drinking companion is more likely to read your mind intuitively and quickly than is a stranger off the street. Do not overlook nepotism, for it can be a good base for empathy. Yet empathy without trust is dangerous, for it can be used against you. Again, it is more difficult to trust a stranger than someone whom you, or your friends, have known for a long time. Selection to club cultures is usually preceded by an introduction and is often confirmed by a meal. You know your friends at the table.

These cultures, then, are clubs of like-minded people introduced by like-minded people, working on empathetic initiative with personal contact rather than formal liaison. They are tough clubs, because if empathy or trust is seen to be misplaced, the man must go. Weak clubs cannot survive because they either must inject other methods of communication (and so lose speed) or risk making too many mistakes.

Club cultures are cheap to run. Trust is cheaper than control procedures, and empathy costs nothing. Money is channeled to where it matters, to people and the promotion of personal contact. Indeed, the telephone and travel bills of these cultures are very high, for Zeus does not write when he can talk. Club cultures are effective when speed is more important than correct detail, or the cost of a delay is higher than the cost of a mistake (which can often be rectified by a subsequent deal). They are good cultures to work in—provided you belong to the club—because they value the individual, give him free rein, and reward his efforts.

Club cultures make history, and Zeus figures are the managers that journalists love most. (Most organizations started as club cultures, and many have not changed when they should have, for speed of decision and the personal imprint of the leader usually become less important as the organization reaches its first plateau of routine.) These cultures depend on networks of friendship, old boys, and comrades and can appear, therefore, to be nepotistic, closed shops, unpopular in these days of meritocracy and equal opportunity. They smack of paternalism and the cult of the individual, of personal ownership and personal power, of the kinds of things that gave the industrial revolution a bad name. They are unfashionable cultures and derided as examples of amateur management and relics of privilege. They should not be. Of course these methods of managing can be abused and often have been—an evil Zeus does evil things—but these organizational squirearchies are very effective in the right situation, for trust based on personal contact is not a bad way of getting things done.

The Role Culture (Apollo) 🏛

When we think of an organization, it is usually the *role* culture that we envisage. It is a culture that bases its approach on the definition of the role or the job to be done, not on personalities.

Apollo is its patron god, for he was the god of order and rules. This culture assumes that man is rational and that everything can and should be analyzed in a logical fashion. The task of an organization can then be subdivided box by box until you have an organizational flow chart of work, with a system of prescribed roles (specified in things called *job descriptions*), which is held together by a set of rules and procedures (call them manuals, budgets, information systems, or what you will).

The role culture's symbol is a Greek temple, for Greek temples draw their strength and their beauty from their pillars. The pillars represent the functions and divisions in a role organization. The pillars are joined managerially only at the top, the pediment, where the heads of the functions and divisions join together to form the board, management committee, or president's office. The pillars are also linked by tension wires of rules and procedures. A typical career would involve joining one of the pillars and working up to the top, with perhaps occasional sightseeing visits to the other pillars ("to broaden one's base"). It is a picture of a bureaucracy, if you like, but *bureaucracy* has come to be a contaminated word, and this culture has its merits.

The Apollo style is excellent when one can assume that tomorrow will be like yesterday. Yesterday can then be examined, pulled to pieces, and put together again in the form of improved rules and procedures for tomorrow. *Stability* and *predictability* are assumed and encouraged. And thank God for them. That the sun will rise tomorrow can be a most reassuring recollection in some of the bleak moments of the late night. Whenever, therefore, the assumptions of stability are valid, it makes sense to codify the operation so that it follows a set and predictable pattern. Individuals are usually indispensable to the operation of the pattern, although as technology advances, more and more stability can be automated. Individuals in the role culture are, therefore, part of the machine, the interchangeable human parts of Henry Ford's dream. The *role,* the set of duties, is fixed. The individual is he, or she, who is slotted into it. That the individual has a name is irrelevant; a number would do as well. That he has a personality is downright inconvenient, because he might then be tempted to express his personality in his role and so alter the role. And that would throw the whole precise logic of the operation out of gear. In a role culture, you do your job, neither more nor less. Efficiency is getting the train in on time, not early and not late. Efficiency is meeting standard targets. Beat them, and it must be assumed that the targets needed revising.

"An interchangeable human part." It sounds deadening. "The occupant of a role" sounds like a sort of organizational squatter. To many, the pure role culture is a denial of humanity because of its insistence on conformity. But to others, it is blessed release.

How pleasant it can be to know exactly what is required of one. How relaxing it sometimes is to be anonymous; how pleasurable not to have to exercise one's initiative, leaving all that creative energy for the home or the community or the sports field.

The Apollo culture is secure psychologically and, usually, contractually. Apollo was a kind god in ancient Greece, the protector of children and sheep as well as of order. Once you join your Greek temple, you can nearly always rely on staying there for life. After all, the temple assumes that it will be there and may even have a twenty-year forecast of what it, and even you, will be doing. The temple will take over your work life for you, and tell you what to do, where to go, and what you can earn. It may even arrange your insurance for you, provide a house or a car, and make cheap shopping or legal advice available. It can and will do some or all of these things because of its assumptions about the predictability of the future.

It is no accident, therefore, that life insurance companies are an example of an almost pure role culture. The notion of predictability is built into the whole ethos of their work. Monopolies, including the civil service, state industries, and local government, can reasonably assume predictability, too, since there is no competition around to disturb their vision of the future. Organizations with a long history of continued success with one product or service or tradition can also be forgiven for thinking that things will continue as before. And if that is so, then the more you rationalize, codify, or standardize, the more effective you will be. If you have the same set of menus for breakfast, lunch, and supper every day, the catering operation in your home will be greatly simplified; the costs of labor and materials will be lower; and the managerial energy required will be minimal. It may be boring, of course, but if food is not enjoyment but only the necessary fuel of life, you will find Apollonian catering.

Apollo cultures are efficient when life is predictable. They hate the obverse—change. They usually respond to a changing environment first by ignoring it and then by doing more of what they are already doing. Responses tend to be stylized in these cultures. When costs go up, Apollo cultures raise the prices or the fares. If sales are flagging, they sell harder. If the backlog of administration is getting too long, they will work more overtime. Greek temples are built on firm ground. If the ground starts to shake, the pillars will quiver and have to be bonded together. If they aren't, the pediment will fall. Translating the analogy, role cultures respond to drastic changes in the environment (changing consumer preferences, new technologies, new funding sources) by setting up a lot of cross-functional liaison groups in an attempt to hold the structure together. If these measures don't work, the management will fall, or the whole temple will collapse in merger, bankruptcy, or a consultants' reorganization.

Zeus or Apollo?

I once worked in a Greek temple organization. It was safe and predictable and promised a secure career. But to me, at age twenty-eight, it was boring. An acquaintance to whom I complained about my condition said, "Why not come and join us? We are looking for an economist to do our project analysis."

"Who is 'us'?" I asked. "An investment bank," he replied, "specializing in the developing countries." "But I'm not an economist," I told him, "I teach philosophy at a university."

"Ah! But it is the right university, isn't it?" he asked, as if that made it all all right. "Come and have lunch with the board on Tuesday."

I had lunch. We talked long about many things—politics, sports, the world. No one mentioned the job, or economics, or my previous experience. Next week they offered me the job of economist, a new post. Two months later I joined them.

They gave me a fine office, a nice secretary, and the *Financial Times*—and then left me alone. Nobody phoned, no memos, letters, nothing. After a week I went to see my friend.

"It's very nice to be here—" I began.

"Good to have you," he replied.

"But . . . " I began.

"Well?"

"I wonder if I could see my job description, get an idea of my role and responsibilities, reporting relationships, and the general organization structure."

"What on earth are you jabbering about, old boy?" he asked, looking startled and worried. "We don't use those sorts of words here—what's worrying you?"

"What am I supposed to be doing?" I blurted out.

"Why, what the rest of us do," he answered. "Search out opportunities to use our resources, get on planes, go and meet people, find some hot news; you know the kind of thing we're interested in, get some more of it."

I returned to my office, alarmed for myself and for them. But then I thought I saw it. They had wanted an economist because they were secretly very worried about this slapdash way of doing things. Clearly, some serious professional project appraisal was urgently needed. Luckily, I just happened to have brought along with me from my previous organization a set of procedures and tables for project appraisal. I could readily adapt these, and then I could propose introducing a little more system and procedure into the current craziness.

In a week I was ready. The chairman arranged for me to present my ideas to a meeting of the board. They all listened very attentively and politely.

At the end, the chairman thanked me for all the work I had put into it and then observed, "I suppose a project would have to be very marginal to justify all this analysis and procedure?"

"Well," I said, "it's obviously vital to marginal propositions, but you can't even know if it's marginal until you've done this kind of formal analysis."

"Hmm. You see, we're probably wrong" (in the tone of voice that Englishmen use when they know they're not), "but in this group we've always thought that we got success not by making *better* decisions on *marginal* propositions than our competitors did, but by making *quicker* decisions on *obvious* propositions."

I defended myself, but I knew that he was right. They were brokers trading in companies. Speed was vital; the accuracy of a decision was only relative. They were Zeus. I was Apollo.

I never did get into their club. In the end, I realized that I had a different cast of mind and left before they threw me out.

The Task Culture (Athena)

The culture of Athena takes a very different approach to management. It sees management as being basically concerned with the continuous and successful solution of problems. First it defines the problem; then allocates to its solution the appropriate resources; gives the resulting group of men, machines, and money the go-ahead; and waits for the solution. It judges performance in terms of results, or solved problems.

The symbol of the task culture is a net because it draws resources from various parts of the organizational system in order to focus them on a particular knot or problem. Power lies at the interstices of the net, not at the top, as in the Apollo culture, or at the center, as in Zeus organizations. Rather, the Athena organization is a network of loosely linked *commando units,* each unit being largely self-contained but having a specific responsibility within an overall strategy.

Its god (or goddess) is a young woman, Athena, the warrior goddess, patroness of Odysseus, arch problem solver of craftsmen and pioneering captains. The culture recognizes only expertise as the base of power or influence. Not age, length of service, or closeness of kin to the owner impresses. To contribute to your group, you need talent, creativity, a fresh approach, and new intuitions. It is a culture in which youth flourishes and creativity is at a premium. The youth, energy, and creativity associated with Athena fit the task culture quite well.

It is a good culture to work in if you know your job. Since the group has a common purpose (the solution of a problem), there is a sense of enthusiasm and joint commitment, with few of the private agenda conflicts that beset the first two cultures. Leadership in a common-purpose group is seldom a hot issue; instead, there is usually mutual respect, a minimum of procedural niceties, and a desire to help rather than exploit when others get into difficulties. It is a *purposeful commando*. It talks of *teams*, whereas a role culture has *committees*.

Task Cultures in Bloom

A friend, employed as an executive with a venerable and traditional British heavy engineering company, went on a working visit to one of the aerospace companies of Southern California, toward the end of the 1960s, when the space race was at its height and the U.S. Defense Department was the world's largest customer, commissioning a long succession of solutions to high-technology problems, often on a cost-plus basis.

Although he did not know it, the aerospace companies at that time were the epitome of the successful task culture. Often as many as 30 percent of their managers had Ph.Ds. Their formal organizational structures were of the matrix type. They worked in project groups that were continually being dismantled and reassembled. They were at that time financially ebullient.

My friend returned to Britain with his eyes gleaming. "It was extraordinary," he said. "In those companies, not only did the sun shine all day outside, but the managers were young, intelligent, earning high salaries, *and* having fun, and the organization made money. In my company," he said ruefully, "we believe that these things are incompatible."

This is the ideal. It works well—indeed, excellently—when the product of the organization is the *solution to a problem*. Consultancy companies, research and development departments, advertising agencies—after all, an advertisement is a response to a client's expressed need—all are one-time problem-solving factories. But put a task culture into a repetitive situation, and there will be trouble. Variety, not predictability, is the yeast of this kind of management. Ask Athenians to manufacture pencils, and they will invent the best (and most expensive?) pencil known, disrupt the process, or depart.

Task cultures are expensive. They are staffed by experts who can demand their market price. They talk together a lot, and talking costs money. Problems are not always solved just right the first time, so there is the necessity for experimentation and the inevitability of errors. Errors cost money, even if they are speedily corrected. Expensive task cultures, therefore, tend to flourish in times of expansion, when the products, technologies, or services are new or when there is some sort of cartel arrangement that provides a price floor. In times of expansion you can get away with high prices—there is more than enough cake to go around. Similarly, new technologies or new products create, for a time, a sort of monopoly situation that lasts until the technology settles down or competitors arrive. During this monopoly situation, the costs or the task structure can be covered by higher charges and prices. In short, task cultures work well when one is venturing into new situations. Luckily, it is in those situations that success is rewarded with the money to pay for it.

Come hard times, however, or an end to venturing, or the need to make the solutions permanent or routine, and the task culture will seem unduly expensive. These cultures are not for plateaus. Athena did not care for domesticity and the routine chores of housekeeping. So task cultures often have a short life. If they are too successful, they will grow big and, to pay their way will take on a lot of routine or maintenance work, which requires Apollonian cultures. Failure, however, is one problem they find it hard to solve (it is hard for a cooperative group to dismiss half its members), and in hard times a Zeus usually emerges to deal with the crisis. Or the members may just grow older and want more routine or more personal power.

Athena in a Storm

Ten years ago, the advertising business in Europe was thriving. Advertising agencies competed strenuously, but on quality and service, not on price, which was still fixed as a standard percentage of the cost (effectively a cost-plus system). The agencies were full of well-paid creative talent, usually young.

I was asked to look at the management process of one agency. It was a model task culture. The whole place was a network of temporary project groups (called *accounts*), pulling in the individual resources from the specialist functions. Most people worked on three or more accounts. Strict standards were applied to the end products (the advertisements), but control and systemization of the means were minimal. How and when the groups worked were left to them. The allocation of personnel to groups was virtually the only managerial task retained in the center. Salaries were high but based on expertise, as recognized by the marketplace (there was a lot of mobility between agencies). There was very little formal hierarchy, but an informal class system based on renown, not closely associated with age. Money was not a crucial factor, for it was always there. Success was measured by public approval, which meant new clients clamoring at the door. The place resembled a luxurious art school, where everyone seemed to be earning vast sums for indulging in his or her hobby. *Management* was, in fact, not a word that was used or a concept that was wanted.

Two years later, world recession, inflation, and tightened company budgets had knocked the bottom right out of the advertising market while hitting the agencies' most vulnerable cost factor, the salaries of their people, their human assets. Agencies began to compete on price. Companies demanded better and quicker service at less cost. Costs had to be controlled, since the business could no longer operate on a cost-plus basis in an expanding market.

Budgets, computer printouts of individual expenses, management committees, redundancy, reductions in office space, a freeze on salaries, lowered mobility, the beginnings of staff unionization—the symptoms were numerous. When I revisited the agency, the task culture was gone. Accounts were administered. Procedures abounded. People talked about "the management," and indeed, the top personnel had changed, to bring in a more managerially minded group, who talked about profit margins, cost effectiveness, and systems. Errors could not be afforded and so were controlled for and eliminated—but so were the experiments that accompanied them. Conformity and predictability had begun to flavor the advertisements. They no longer made bad ads, but some thought they no longer made great ones, either.

Suddenly it was just like another business. The art school had become an ad factory. The task culture was now a role culture with a few Zeus figures at the top.

Necessary? Perhaps. Sad? Certainly. Task cultures don't easily weather storms.

The Existential Culture (Dionysus)

Dionysus, god of wine and song, presides over this culture because he, if anyone, represents the existential ideology among the gods. Existentialism starts from the assumption that the world is *not* some part of a higher purpose; we are not simply instruments of some god. Instead, although the fact that we exist at all is an accident, if anyone is responsible for us and our world, it is ourselves. We are in charge of our own destinies. This is not a recipe for self-indulgent selfishness, for Kant's categorical imperative applies: that whatever we ordain or wish for ourselves must be equally applicable to the rest of humankind. Wine and orgies won't work unless someone makes the wine, and that someone must potentially include us.

The organizational implications of existential thinking are great. In the other three cultures, the individual is subordinate to the organization: The style of the relationship may vary, but the individual is there to help the organization achieve its purpose and is paid in one way or another by the organization for doing that. In this fourth existential culture, the organization exists to help the individual achieve his purpose.

How does this happen? Well, think of doctors: four of them, each an individual with his own speciality but who agree to share an office, a telephone, and a secretary to form a partnership association. Or think of architects or lawyers, or a cooperative of artists. Theirs is a communal culture, existing only for its participants. Its picture is a cluster of individual stars loosely gathered in a circle. But the picture will remain essentially unchanged even if a star or two departs. The stars are not mutually interdependent.

The existential culture is excellent, therefore, when it is the talent or skill of the individual that is the crucial asset of the organization.

This is the culture preferred by professionals. They can preserve their own identity and their own freedom, feeling owned by no one. And yet they can be part of an organization, with the colleagues, the support, and the added flexibility, and even the bargaining power that association brings.

Dionysians recognize no "boss," although they may accept co-ordination for their own long-term convenience. Management in their organizations is a chore, something that has to be done like housekeeping. And like a housekeeper, a manager has small renown: An administrator among the prima donnas is at the bottom of the status lists.

Dionysian cultures are splendid places to work in. I have worked in one myself—a university. Professionals usually have job security, agreed fee scales, allocated territories or spheres of influence, and guarantees of independence. This is marvelous for them, but not for those who have to lead or organize or manage such people.

For there are no sanctions that can be used on them. Dismissal, money, perks, or punishment all are outside the jurisdiction of the leader. Even promotion or selection decisions are made, as a rule, by groups of equals. Professionals do not willingly take orders, fill in forms, or compromise on their own plans. Every teacher likes to be the uninterrupted king in his own classroom, just as every doctor is the god of his consulting room. You enter by invitation only, criticize on request, and command by consent. For these are the organizations of consent, in which the manager governs with the consent of the governed and not with the delegated authority of the owners. It may be democracy, but it is very difficult and exhausting to deal with such a culture.

One would not expect to find many such organizations around, certainly not in business or industry, where organizations, because of their charters, have objectives that outlive and outgrow their employees. Indeed, the Dionysian culture causes shudders in the ordinary organization or manager, precisely because of the lack of mandated control. When you can manage only by consent, every individual has the right of veto, and so any coordinated effort becomes a matter of endless negotiation. Only when every person can do what he wants, and could in fact operate without the organization at all, are there fewer problems. Antique hypermarkets, in which individual dealers ply their trades independently, although under one roof—a marketing cooperative for independent growers or craftsmen—can usually be managed (though they would not use the word) without too much difficulty. There would be few conflicting objectives, few needs to compromise individual desires for a common good.

Organizations, however, put the common good before the individual need, and so they tend to try to translate Dionysians into Athenians, the existential into the task culture. They are, of course, right, as judged by their own interests, to try to do so. Individuals, however, like the notions of individuality and personal professionalism that reside in the Dionysian idea. There is a growing band of "new professionals"—individuals who define themselves according to their trade, not just doctors and lawyers, but now also the "systems analyst," "research scientist," "public relations adviser," and "consultant." These people see themselves as independent professionals who have temporarily lent their talents to an organization. They are often young and usually talented and can command an open market salary and reputation. They behave like Dionysians, and as long as they are talented, they can get away with it, for the organization needs them enough to manage them on the terms of their consent. Increasingly, therefore, the specialist groups and any research or development activities are acquiring an existential flavor.

Whenever individual talent is at a premium, the Dionysian flavor is probably necessary, and organizations do well to recognize it and accommodate it. But the cult of Dionysus is growing and is no longer related to individual talent. We all would like the benefits of existentialism without its responsibilities and risks. Existentialism on the shop floor is a new phenomenon. We shall return to this in the second part of this book.

Family Cultures

Have families changed their cultures?

Once upon a time, the paterfamilias ruled as Zeus over his table. He was master, and all knew it. They did as he commanded when he commanded.

Then Apollo became the fashion: To each his duties and his status. The men made the money; women the food; children the beds.

Democracy brought Athena into the family. Not duties but tasks, projects, and small-group activities became its defining feature. "Why don't you both . . . ?" or "Shall we . . . ?"

And now Dionysus? A temporary liaison of persons. If individual interests start to diverge, the liaison cannot be enforced. Joint activities (e.g., holidays) cannot be assumed or imposed, only negotiated.

Do organizations follow a similar sort of cultural inevitability? If so, where are we on the progression?

Which Are You?

You probably do not identify completely with any of the four gods. Most people, the Greeks included, are too complex to do that and so pay homage to more than one philosophy. Similarly, your organization probably includes aspects of all four cultures.

Do my classifications apply to your experience? Only you can judge that for yourself, but in his study of the ways of U.S. corporations, Michael Maccoby produced his own four classes of organizational characters:[1]

> *The Jungle Fighter:* His goal is power. He experiences life and work as a jungle, where winners destroy the losers. There are two subtypes, the lion and the fox, different in the way they walk their jungles.
>
> *The Company Man:* His sense of identity is based on being part of the powerful protective company. He is concerned with the human side of the company; his interest is in the feelings of the people around him; but he also has a commitment to maintain the organization's integrity.
>
> *The Gamesman:* The gamesman is the new man. His main interest is in a challenging competitive activity. He enjoys new ideas,

new techniques, fresh approaches. He is a team player, playing for the corporation.

The Craftsman: His interest is in the *process* of making something, in doing a craftsmanlike job. Many scientists in organizations fall into this category. They want to do their own thing rather than to master or manage the system.

The resemblance to the four Greek gods is unmistakable.

There is, too, some historical significance in the order in which I have placed the gods. Most organizations originated as club cultures, almost squirearchies built around the personality of the founder, the owner, or the patriarch. These are the traditional tribes—the first form of organization, I suppose, informal, intuitive, and personal. This form of Zeus management lasted for a long, long time. Take even the railways of England, built in the nineteenth century, incredible examples not only of engineering but also of coordinated manual effort, in which over 200,000 men were at one time working with pick and shovel: Even their organization was based on subcontracting to gangs of unskilled laborers working for a Zeus figure. It was the introduction of the factory that changed things, with the idea that work could be broken down into its component parts rather than multiplied out, so that, instead of having one hundred gangs working on one hundred different engines, you divided up segments of the engine. This change in the technology of work required rules and procedures—the role culture. The role culture produced enormous cost reductions when linked to the new self-powered technology of steam and then electricity. It turned out, however, to be a very expensive culture for one-time jobs and to be slow at reacting to the unexpected.

The committee of experts, on the other hand, had always been around. But it was not until the pace of change speeded up that it began to be a widely used basis for management, called a *project team* or *task force.* As it is so often, it was probably the innovative pressures of war that fostered the task culture as a method of organization.

Now, today, the increased specialization of technology is beginning to make Dionysians of us all. The idea that armies, for instance, will soon be just groups of scientists is not such a remote possibility.

If you examine the history of most organizations, you will find that they have progressed through the club (Zeus) culture to the role (Apollo) culture, to which they have subsequently added the task (Athenian) and existential (Dionysian) cultures as they have needed to change and develop. By now, most organizations of any size are some mix of all four.

Organizations, however, need to do more than merely equip themselves with a mix of cultures and their attendant gods. The cultures must first be internally consistent, for Apollonian assumptions of order and rationality cannot produce results in the task culture (Athenian) part of the organization, or vice versa. Second, of course, you need the right culture for the right job: A club (Zeus) culture for the accounts department would nearly always be inefficient. These are the two most common causes of mixed-up management, and we shall examine them later. Meantime, the Dinner Party Game may enliven the occasional boring evening.

The Dinner Party Game

Try this rudimentary form of cultural diagnosis when at your next party. Ask your neighbor what he does for a living.

If he replies, "I work for X," naming a person whom you are supposed to have heard of, he will turn out to be in a Zeus culture.

If he says, "I work with Y company or organization," going on perhaps, to define his job title, he will be in an Apollonian role culture.

If he gives his title first and then his organization, as for example, "I am in marketing, with W. company," then he probably sees his part of the organization, and himself, as a task culture.

If he just says, "I am a lawyer" or "I paint," he is a Dionysian.

The Mix of Differences

Why would these very different gods be required in the same organization? Well, looked at in one way, life is just a set of jobs to be done. Organizations are just larger sets of jobs to be done.

These jobs seem to fall into three types: steady-state, development, and asterisk.

Let me explain.

Steady-state describes those jobs that are programmable because they are predictable. They can be handled by systems and routines, by rules and procedures. In a typical organization, they might actually account for 80 percent of the quantity of work to be done.

Development jobs are those that attempt to deal with new situations or problems. In many cases, the result may be a new system or routine, which ensures that the next time the event occurs it will not be a problem but merely an incident in the steady-state. These are the jobs that ensure, if they are well done, that the organization will adapt. In many organizations, the groups responsible for them include the word *development* in their title (as in Product Development or Systems Development).

Not all problems are development jobs, however. Some are what I can best describe as *Asterisk* situations. Asterisk situations are the exceptions, the occasions when the rules have failed, the emergencies in which instinct and speed are likely to be better than logical analysis or creative problem solving. These situations must be resolved by personal intervention.

Each of these job types has its matching symbol and its god. If the wrong god is matched to the wrong job, it will cause mixed-up management and its consequence, inefficiency.

The steady-state is a square

,

and Apollo, of the role culture, is its god.

Development activities require a creative cell,

and Athena is their goddess, with her problem-solving capacity.

Asterisk situations are represented, naturally, by an asterisk *, and here Zeus and Dionysus share the honors (a liaison that has caused some confusion).

"Management" happens when these activities are linked together in an appropriate fashion and are given some common purpose or direction. See art below.

The "manager" therefore must embody all four cultures. He must be able to emulate each god in the appropriate circumstances. If you want an explanation for the lure of management, this is it—the simultaneous call of four gods. And if managers look weary, well they might after this quadruple culture shock—cultural schizophrenia.

Most people can't do it, of course. Most people revert, particularly when tired or stressed, to their favorite culture. So organizations, which are made up of managers and managees, after all, tend to become culture bound. When individuals or organizations become culture bound, they start to define jobs to fit their cultural inclinations. Zeus characters see development problems as asterisk situations calling for their personal intervention. Apollonians try to make everything fit the rules even if that is obviously the most complicated way of doing it. Athenians love creation. They are prone to inventing fine solutions to unnecessary problems (the "Concorde" phenomenon) or to devising answers that, though immaculate, are hugely expensive to implement. To be adequate is not a challenge to Athenians, only to Apollonians. Mixed-up management.

Zeus in the Carpet Warehouse

My wife has, in her time, worked as an interior designer and decorator. She used, then, to complain that the problems of management did not require the complex and elaborate theories of management academics for their solution. "Common sense," she observed, "is all that anyone needs, and the ability to read and write." "Consider,"

she would say, "the carpet problems that I have. Last week I ordered a red carpet to be sent on Tuesday to Kingston. Instead, they sent a *blue* carpet on *Thursday* to *Richmond*. No great problem for me," she added. "I found Fred up in the warehouse, cursed him, and chatted him up. 'That's all right, luv,' he assured me. 'Bill will get the van out, pick up the blue carpet, bring it back here, and get your red carpet to your customer by this afternoon.' And so they did. They always get it right the second time. But the cost to them must be tremendous. Efficiency just means getting it right the first time."

She was right, of course. But getting it right the first time would mean a system of checks and controls, matching orders to delivery orders to truck schedules to calendars dates. All very straightforward but involving bits of paper and files and checks. Boring stuff, at least for Fred, who has been running the warehouse for thirty years and likes to keep everything in his own head. That way, he can spend his day giving orders, dealing with questions, settling disputes, placating angry customers, and allocating drivers, all by personal intervention. His idea of bliss is to have three telephones ringing, one face at the window, and another at the door, all needing him, at once. *Then* he feels indispensable, powerful, valuable.

He is a Zeus sabotaging the steady-state. An asterisk in a square. A mismatch of cultures equals expense, in this case Bill running unnecessary errands in his van.

So it is that organizations often, even usually, end up with the wrong cultures in the wrong places, with jobs defined by favorite gods rather than gods assigned to jobs. Even in our daily lives as individuals, we are guilty of this theistic favoritism. As a confirmed Dionysian with streaks of Athena, I cannot find it in my heart to do the routine tasks of household maintenance, which I designate as *suburban trivialities*. Inevitably, our house is prone to endless emergencies calling for creative solutions and personal inspiration. The steady-state is minimal, and asterisks and cells abound.

More instances of mixed-up management:

• Developmental cells may be required to solve the coordination problems of the steady-state, with all its systems. If they don't, then asterisk situations will arise, and Zeus-style action will be needed. Too much of this, however, and the steady-state will become pitted with cells and asterisks, depriving it of much of its strength. Reverting to earlier symbols, the pillars of the temple are affected by a sort of cultural dry rot. A plethora of projects is a danger sign in a Greek temple organization.

• In an attempt to minimize costs, Apollo organizations may attempt to standardize and systematize everything, even developmental jobs. An Apollonian tends to use the past to forecast the future. Apollonian planning, for instance, is a euphemism for "projections." Initiative is then stifled by "proper channels," and the energies of the Athenian or Zeus characters are diverted into beating the system.

• In the 1980s, it was fashionable for large organizations to have corporate planning departments. In many cases, these rightly became creative cells with an Athenian task culture. Staffed by young, talented, and enthusiastic individuals, scenarios, alternative futures, and forecasts poured out of them. Unfortunately, these had often little impact on the mainstream organization (the steady-state of manufacturing and marketing or of administration and services). The cells were rather like hornet's nests hanging from the gutters of the Greek temple. Often the departments were housed, territorially, at the edge of the headquarters' building and were attached, structurally, to the management through the most junior directors. Often they found it easier to communicate with other creative cells, even those in competing organizations (at conferences or courses or conventions), than with their own steady-state colleagues. But this "organizational irrelevance" made it easier to amputate the cells when economic stringency was needed in later years.

• In a competitive talent hunt, large organizations try to restock their manpower bank with an annual intake of young graduates, MBAs, or professionals. Rightly or wrongly, these people have often been educated in a problem-solving mode, that is, the Athenian task culture. If the interest and commitment of these individuals are to be retained, they need to work on developmental tasks in problem-solving cells. But for many organizations, the key managerial posts lie in the steady-state. The transference is not easy. Athenian notions of project teams, participative management, and every man an expert can actually get in the way of routines and administration. The alternative—putting in the young Athenians as apprentices at the bottom of the steady-state pillars ("get their hands dirty," "learn the ropes the hard way," "a few months on the road never did anyone any harm")—can be a huge culture shock to the new recruit, breeding a disillusionment with life in organizations that he may never get over.

Asterisk situations are interesting ones. They properly occur where you might least expect them: not at the *top* of organizations but in the *middle*. At the top, the decisions have long-term implications: They are developmental problems that are more appropriately and productively solved by Athenian cells. Asterisk situations usually are created by dilemmas in human relationships, which are, of all situations, the least amenable to prediction or programming. Personal conflicts, imminent disputes, intergroup rivalries, private crises, crucial selection, or promotion decisions—these are the sparks that start an asterisk job. Of course, they can occur in the boardroom or the council chamber as well as in the factory or office, but numerically and proportionately they will be less significant. It is at the supervisor and middle-management level that Zeus should reign, or out on the road where the salesman or driver must act on his own and use his initiative when the rules run out. Unhappily, it is at the middle and edges of organizations that Zeus figures are least tolerated. They are most numerous at the top, although times are changing in some organizations, in which the idea of president's office, a triumvirate or quadrumvirate of top talent acting as a team (or cell), is becoming more common, as an adaptive recognition that the prime task of the directorate is one of development, not of personal intervention. (There remain, of course, the ritual and ambassadorial duties of a tribal head. A Zeus figure is appropriate here, to represent the organization on formal or external occasions, as a sort of constitutional monarch.)

Differences, then, are necessary and good for organizational health. Monotheism, the pursuit of a single god, is wrong for most organizations. But the choice and blend of gods cannot be haphazard, for the wrong god in the wrong place means pain and inefficiency.

2

The Gods
at Work

You have now been introduced to the current gods of our organizations. An introduction is, however, only an invitation to get better acquainted. One would be foolish, on the basis of so short an acquaintance, to start restructuring one's organization. The ways of each culture need further exploration and explanation should anyone want to act on them. Our next tasks will be to unravel the differences among the cultures and then to suggest how the cultures can be knitted together again to make up the balanced and efficient organization that would solve the first level of problem in our organized society.

Balance and efficiency eliminate *slack*. Slack in an organization means a waste of resources, be those resources money, people, or materials. Slack is today the slow cancer of our organized society; and it is explained in more detail later.

I have argued that each organization needs a mix of cultures, a different culture or god for each major activity, process, or job. But within each activity or section of the organization, cultural purity should prevail. The cultures must be internally consistent, for even though organizations need more than one god, individuals are monotheists; they want one god at a time, cultural purity.

Apollonians at Work

Apollonian assumptions, for instance, applied to Athenian individuals produce resentment, cynicism, and reluctant conformity, like the signs of guilt in an individual who knows that he denies himself. A healthy organization is therefore one that is culturally true in its parts. Where Apollo is needed and where Apollonians work, Apollonian ways are healthy. But if the work demands Apollo and your people are Dionysians, what then? Do you change your clothes to suit your job or change your job to suit your clothes? Which is an organization's true culture? The one that the logic of the work demands or the one that exists in the individuals and their cultures?

Each culture makes its own assumptions about how individuals think and learn, can be influenced, may be changed, or might be motivated. These assumptions result in theories and practices of individual development and, in philosophies of change, systems of control, and mechanisms of reward. But what works in one culture does not work, or does not work so well, in another. Cultural harmony is health as well as happiness. Fashion, that insidious agent of change, may bring management by objectives, appraisal, or team building into vogue. All these, however, are mechanisms best suited to their own culture. Transplanted to another, they are ineffective, or worse, they generate artificial behavior, the rituals and rites of organizations that so often are the outward signs of corporate malaise. Without cultural awareness, organizations too easily find themselves genuflecting to false gods. The only universal sin, it is held, is to be untrue to oneself. Organizational "sin" is committed when a culture is untrue to itself. We shall look, then, at each culture in turn, at its assumptions and practices in the three critical areas of thinking and learning, influencing and changing, and motivating and rewarding.

The Club Culture (Zeus)

Ways of Thinking and Learning

Zeus individuals tend to think intuitively and in wholes. They move fast to a possible solution and test it, moving to another if the first solution looks unsuitable. A logical step-by-step analysis is not their way, for they like responding to stimulus and get bored easily. Thus they like a jumble of events (nine-minute shots, as one research study shows), and days that are full of variety. They rely a lot on impressionistic, "soft" data and set little store by the conventional hard data of reports and analyses. They think holistically or in totals, seeing the full picture and assessing it, instead of building it up bit by bit from its parts.

Chief Executives in Action

Henry Mintzberg watched five chief executives at work and concluded the following:[1]

1. The chief executives strongly favored verbal communication rather than written communication.

2. Analytical inputs—reports, documents, budgets—seemed of relatively little importance to these chief executives. They attached more weight to soft and speculative data—impressions and feelings, hearsay, gossip. Given these data, they *synthesized* rather than *analyzed*.

3. The chief executive is usually the best-informed member of the organization but has difficulty in disseminating that information to the rest of the organization, perhaps because his information is "soft," intuitive, and not formalized.

4. The chief executives had a simultaneous, experimental, hectic, unplanned work pattern. Half their activities were completed in less than nine minutes; there were no evident patterns in their days; they preferred interruption (leaving meetings, keeping doors open); and they disliked routine (only 7 percent of their verbal contacts were regularly scheduled).

5. *Leader, disturbance handler,* and *liaison man* were the words that best described their main roles.

6. In only fourteen of twenty-five decision processes observed was there an explicit diagnosis stage. Instead, chief executives preferred to jump straight to the solution.

7. Timing was of great importance in the chief executive's assessment of actions.

8. In only eighteen of eighty-three choices made by the chief executives did they mention using explicit analysis. *Intuition* and *judgment* better describe what they did.

This Zeus-like behavior is typical of many chief executives. The question we must ask is whether it is appropriate at the top of that organization.

Zeus individuals do not learn logically or analytically or sequentially; rather, they learn by *trial and error* or by *modeling*. And that is how they expect others to learn. The methods of training and development that Zeus cultures apply to their youth can be labeled *apprenticeship* methods: "Work with me for a while, see how I do it, and when I think it's right, I will let you try." In Zeus cultures, one finds systems of personal assistants or a chief executive's cadre of young hopefuls. People speak of protégés and crown princes, of heirs to the succession, who will be tested at some organizational proving grounds, by giving them their own small commands in which they will be free to demonstrate their ability without causing too much damage to the parent concern. It is possible to succeed while still young in these cultures, given a strong patron and success in early trials. Choosing one's models is perhaps the key to successful learning, for one then models the kinds of behavior and values that lead to success in that business or trade or profession.

The senior figures in a Zeus culture find their models in other organizations. A Zeus person does not inquire. "What is current theory?" but, rather, "What is so-and-so doing?" She uses the luncheon tables of conferences and the receptions of society to unearth new models for her own development. Above all, to Zeus people, learning must be secret. To a Zeus person, an admission of a need to learn is an admission of a deficiency. I was once asked to advise the Zeus-type board of an organization: "But come after the office closes," they said, "and use the rear entrance, if you wouldn't mind." A professor on the premises might be an omen of disaster! After all, these are club cultures, clubs in which like learns from like and outsiders have little to contribute.

Ways of Influencing and Changing

In club cultures, it is the control of resources and personal charisma that counts. If you own the club, you can tell people what to do. If you have a track record of success, then you have that certain smell called *charisma*. A rather charming piece of leadership theory talks of "idiosyncrasy credits," earning the right to do what you want in the way that you want. But the credits have to be earned, since there can be no overdraft of idiosyncrasy credits, although anyone's bank balance of credits can be used up by too many idiosyncrasies and so need renewal by another run of success. Wise people in Zeus cultures do not overspend their credits.

From those power bases of resources and charisma, the Zeus culture creates change by changing people, for people are the link pieces in these cultures. If a link is failing—replace it. A Zeus thinker instinctively responds to an organizational problem by asking, "Whose job is that? Change him." Change can mean reform or education, but often in these organizations, it literally means replacement. Clubs can be tough, and Zeus cultures do not always respond to the logic of the argument so much as to the signature at its end. "Who said that?" is a more pertinent question than "What was said?" Results speak louder than reasons, and actions than arguments, for you do not change the course of these organizations by reasoning, but by reasons in the mouths of credible persons.

Hence the reputation of Zeus cultures for organization politics. If the source of the argument counts more than its logic, then your choice of individuals and of clubs within clubs will be crucial. You will succeed or not, and be judged, by whom, not what, you know, although whom you know will depend on what you do. Inevitably, these cultures are political. But that word *political* is only a sneer when used by people of other cultures. Zeus people accept and enjoy a world of personalities and power based on credits and ownership.

Credibility Wins

I had been asked to investigate the economics of a possible investment in northwest Africa and to advise the chairman on what action the board should take.

After a week of careful research, two late nights, and much analysis, I produced a report, full of charts, estimates, and calculations. At the front was the mandatory half-sheet of paper with my conclusions, summed up

(conclusively, I thought) in the properly discounted annual rate of return of 15.7 percent after tax. It must be a
good thing.

The chairman looked at it.

"Thank you," he said, "you've put a lot of work into
this. You think we should go ahead?"

"Of course," I said, "no doubt about it."

"I see, I think I'll just have a word with John," said the
chairman (mentioning the name of a well-known merchant banker). He called him on the phone and briefly
described the situation, and there followed a five-minute
conversation of which all that I heard was

"Yes . . . I see . . . Really? . . . Hm . . . Naturally. . . .
Quite so. . . . Thank you very much, John."

He put the phone down.

"No," he said. "It's not on. John says, 'Wrong place,
wrong time, wrong company.' Thanks all the same, old
boy."

I was grossly offended by this victory of old-boy network over rational analysis. In time, however, I came to
recognize that the credibility of John, with much successful experience in overseas investment, was rightly more
important to that Zeus organization than my untested
technical reasoning could be.

Motivating and Rewarding

Zeus characters look for power over people and events. They
like to see things happen as a result of their personal action or
intervention. It is their desire that personally, they should make
a difference.

The implications are fairly clear. They enjoy situations in
which they have a great deal of discretion, in which they have
power over resources, and in which personal intuitive decisions
are important. To be confined in their responsibilities or to pre-
side over an area in which technical expertise alone provides the
answer to the crucial questions are to them constraints on their
potential and therefore de-motivating.

In Zeus cultures, money is highly valued, but it is usually
money as an enabling factor or money as a symbol of results

achieved. Many Zeus people do not spend heavily on personal goods, regarding this as the wasteful use of a means of power. People or information as well as money can be the object of their collector's instinct, as they know intuitively that these commodities are often at least as powerful as money. To this end, they invest considerable time in creating and maintaining *networks*, potential sources of useful people, useful information, or even cash. Such people seldom rest from their labors, because they do not work for rest but for zest: in resting, they might miss an opportunity to make a difference. They like uncertainty (including gambles) because uncertainty implies freedom to maneuver.

It all fits well into the club culture: trust and empathy backing up intuitive decisions, personal charisma based on a track record of success, money as a thermometer of success, and politics, people, and networks as a way of life. Reward these people with responsibility: Give them resources, a challenge, and your trust. Control them by results or the look in their eyes, not by pension schemes or titles or even office cars.

Peter and the Potatoes

After one long hot European summer, potatoes had become expensive in the shops. One Saturday I went shopping with a friend, a successful ship broker, one of those men who was clearly very wealthy but always needed to borrow money, for all his own was committed. We were staggered by the price of potatoes and walked out refusing to buy any.

Two weeks later, I saw him again:

"Remember those potatoes?" he said. "What did you do about them?"

"I went home and decided to buy rice instead," I replied. "Why, didn't you?"

"Oh, no, I rang up a contact in Calcutta, ordered 2,000 tons of Indian potatoes at £100 per ton, arranged freight and insurance for £30 per ton, and sold them in advance to a London merchant I knew for £230 per ton."

"But Peter," I said, "that's £100 per ton profit and on 2,000 tons. . . ."

"Don't worry," he said, smiling, "It didn't come off.

The Indian government stopped the shipment on the docks, but for three phone calls it was worth the chance."

I switched to rice. He nearly made £200,000. But he maintains an extensive network. I would not have known who to call even if I had thought of it. Besides, what would I do with £200,000—invest it? He would have staked it all on another deal.

The Role Culture (Apollo)

The role culture is quite different. Apollonians think differently and therefore make different assumptions about influence, control, and the motivation of others. It may have something to do with which side of the brain developed first, the environment of one's youth, or even the first organization encountered in life. Apollo followers find Zeus people crude, irrational, unpredictable, frightening at times, and certainly different. The two cultures do not mix. A Zeus chafes under an Apollonian regime and forgets to trust his intuition or his network. An Apollo can be useful to a Zeus superior, but his more logical ways must be understood and tolerated by the Zeus figure if his true capacity is to develop.

Are You Right or Left-Brained?

There is an emerging consensus that our talents may have something to do with which side of our brain developed first. Scientists have known for some time that the brain has two distinct hemispheres. In the left hemisphere of most people's brains are located the logical thinking processes. This left side of the brain works sequentially, in a linear manner. Language is one common example. The right hemisphere looks at patterns, complete images, or relationships.

Speech seems to belong to the left side, but movement and emotions to the right, logic to the left, inspiration and creativity to the right. Much of education is linear or sequential or verbal, stimulating the left side but perhaps neglecting the right. Those who are bad at logic may be good at art. Lawyers, scientists, and accountants may have a developed left brain; artists, politicians—and some managers?—a developed right brain.

Henry Mintzberg suggested that successful chief executives rely more on "feel" and intuition than on systematic reasoning (right more than left), that they "synthesize" rather than "analyze," that they know intuitively, more than they can communicate, revel in ambiguity, and dislike regularity.[2] Mintzberg goes on to propose that planning is a left-brained activity, which can be made systematic, but that creative strategy needs right-brain thinking, which usually comes from one person.

Are Apollo and Athena left-brained, Zeus and Dionysus right-brained?

Ways of Thinking and Learning

Apollo definitely prefers the left-hand side of the brain. Apollonian thinking is logical, sequential, analytical. Apollonians would like to believe in a formally scientific world in which events move according to predetermined formulas. They like to proceed from defining the problem to identifying the appropriate solution mechanism ("This is a logistical distribution problem; therefore apply the appropriate operations research technique"). On the whole, the more of these mechanisms you know and can use, the more problems you are likely to be able to deal with. Efficiency tends to mean simplification, getting things down to the bare but essential features.

Intelligence is a useful indicator of ability, but it is intelligence of the convergent rather than the divergent kind—straight rather than lateral thinking.

Learning, therefore, in Apollonian cultures, pertains to the acquisition of more knowledge and skills; it is additive; and it is acquired by a *transfer* process (called *training*), in which those who possess the desired knowledge or skills pass them on to those who don't. It follows that individuals can, to a large extent at least, be classified according to their possession of knowledge, experience (another sort of knowledge), and skills and be allocated to roles that require particular sets of these. If the requisite skill is lacking, it sometimes can, by means of training, be provided.

This way of looking at thinking and learning fits routine predictable activities very well, as these activities can be broken down into sets of required knowledge, skills, and experience. It is therefore in Apollonian cultures that you find individuals spoken of as "human resources"—resources that can be planned, scheduled, deployed, and reshuffled like any other physical asset. To this culture, then, belong the formal techniques of manpower planning: assessment centers, appraisal schemes, training needs diagnosis, training courses, job rotation—in fact, all the paraphernalia of traditional management development.

The contamination arises when these attitudes and approaches are used in other cultures. In fact, in most organizations, these techniques peter out as the higher echelons are reached; for most organizations have a Zeus-cum-Athena culture at the apex, with individuals who have the power to ignore among themselves the rules they set for others. The mechanisms of Apollo are thus often confined to the lower and middle regions. Although many might mutter about one law for the rich and another for the poor, there may be intuitive wisdom in this apparent flouting of democracy.

Ways of Influencing and Changing

It is in Apollonian organizations that *authority* becomes a recognizable concept. "With what authority do you do that?" is a meaningful question in the steady-state, whereas in a Zeus culture it would be seen as ritualistic mumbo jumbo. Power in the role cultures stems from one's role or position or title. Written into that role is a list of rights as well as responsibilities. The organization chart (an indispensable piece of equipment in role cultures, although often unheard-of in club cultures) is a diagrammatic way of showing who can give orders to whom or via whom. If you don't have the title, you can only *ask*, not *tell*. The authority of your position not only entitles you to tell someone to do something; it also allows you to create a complex of rules, procedures, and systems for your own domain. These rules, procedures, and systems are the railways of the steady-state. They direct and steer the flow of information and activities that turn inputs into outputs. And as with railways, the driver (manager) is there to influence the speed, not to control the direction. In an Apollo culture, the manager is the person *in* authority, whereas the Zeus manager *has* authority (his own, not that of the organization).

It is a misconception to believe that managing means decision making in the role culture. Decisions are in fact few in number and are very much of the processing category ("Do we let that go, start this one, direct that one?"). It is the design of the organization's railway system that is crucial: Its operation requires only an adherence to timetables. Administration is a word that fits Apollo cultures but is anathema to Zeus.

It follows that to change Apollonian systems, one must change either the sets of roles and responsibilities (the *structure*) or the network of rules and procedures (the *systems*). Changing any individual (the engine driver) has a minor impact compared with changes in the structure or systems (the lines of track or the timetable). Astute Zeus men trapped in an Apollo culture adapt their own cultural instincts and use the rules and procedures and role descriptions of Apollo to lock in their competitors and to free themselves. In so doing they distort the logic of the organization and so contaminate that culture and their own. This is an example of the unconstructive politics of organizations—the manipulation of the Apollonian systems for personal advantage.

Budgets in Apollo

Budgets in Apollo cultures are one way of defining one's organizational territory and personal discretion. It is tempting to any person of self-conceit to enlarge his domain by bidding for an increased budget. But one person's increase must be another person's decrease, unless an enlarged budget for the total organization is accepted.

An enlarged total budget must, of course, be accompanied by a matching increase in output. If it is not, then organizational inflation will occur, an increase in the "money supply" of the organization without an accompanying increase in productivity. In organizational terms, the "money supply" is activity. Under budget inflation, activity or "busyness" rises, but output remains constant. In physics, this is known as *Brownian motion*.

Apollonians prefer compromise to conflict. The mechanics of compromise breed budget in inflation. It takes a tough and ruthless new arrival, or the imminence of catastrophe, to slash budgets. When they are thriving, Apollo cultures tend therefore to be prone to a creeping inflation, with "activity" increasing faster than output.

Are budgets, one must ask, an underlying cause of the progressive paralysis of large organizations?

Ways of Motivating and Rewarding

Apollo men are tidy men. They value order and predictability in their lives as in their affairs. Things need to fit into place, with contracts precise and honored, roles prescribed and maintained. "Duty" is an important concept to them, as is the notion of obligation, or responsibility to carry out one's own tasks. They are seldom curious, believing that the world around them is mainly organized by people who should know what they are doing (even if the evidence is sometimes lacking!).

It is not easy to describe the motivation of Apollonians without making them seem dull. The reason is that they pursue certainty as avidly as a Zeus person shuns it and that the role, or the job to be done, is at least as important as the deeper purpose behind it all. If it sometimes seems remarkable that life goes on with its sowing and harvesting, buying and selling, fetching and carrying, despite the eruptions of economic crises or armed rebellions, it is Apollonians that we must thank for it. Head down in their role, they prefer to assume the certainty they cannot always see. This gives them a particular slant on life. An Apollonian believes in life insurance and pension funds, confident that life has sufficient predictability for it to be sensible to make long-term provisions for the future. A Zeus sees a pension only as a source of realizable assets. An Apollonian finds sense and security in the budgets and job descriptions of a formal organization, even if he may debate the details, whereas a Zeus views them only as constraints on his opportunism.

Again, these characteristics fit the requirements of the role culture, which relies on predictability to be effective. The complex of long-term careers, pension schemes, career planning, role descriptions, rules, procedures, and operating plans that a role culture needs to do its work all fit the "psychological" contract required by Apollonians. They are very contractual people, in fact, and are more inclined than most to formalize that psychological contract, turning it into a full legal contract in many cases—a tendency that can frustrate the Zeus personalities who often sit at the top of their organizations.

Because Apollonians value the power that is conveyed by the formal authority of their role, they are appropriately rewarded by an increase in formal authority and its outward visible sign, status. It is in role organizations that people most avidly compare and compete for the status symbols of the organized society: the company car, the expense account, the executive suite. It is appropriate that they should, though to another culture this would seem a meaningless and petty game.

The Task Culture (Athena)

The task culture is the culture of the group, the group of experts focusing on a common task or problem. It is the organizational culture that best suits those who have been rationally educated in a democratic society, people who like to think that they are living in a meritocracy and who would not be offended to be called meritocrats themselves. Success, to organizational Athenians, is desirable if it has been earned. Such people regard Zeus people as overprivileged, lucky, or unduly thoughtless. They occasionally may admire the forcefulness of a Zeus but would wish it had been preceded by more counsel and deliberation. Apollonians are seen by Athenians as useful but boring people, desiring to perpetuate the present rather than explore the potential of the future and of change. Most of the new professionals in organizations, those who think of themselves as "marketing men" or "corporate planners" or "product managers" see themselves as task culture people, Athenians. It is, in fact, the form of management that most people accept and aspire to. Unfortunately, as the last chapter indicated, it is an expensive and luxurious way of running organizations, so it is frequently contaminated: A problem solved by Athenians must be administered in Apollonian ways. But the people are often the same, and there lies the rub.

Ways of Thinking and Learning

Athenians are problem solvers. Problems are solved best, they believe, by a mix of creativity with some applied logic. Fundamental, too, to the process of problem solving is the ability to work with others. Many brains make better solutions, as long as they work with, not against or for, one another. Learning, therefore, is acquiring the ability to solve problems better. Some technical aids may help, and a little Apollonian instruction can sometimes be useful, but the crucial learning is by means of continual exploration or discovery, successive problem solving of the hypothesize—test—rehypothesize variety. Mix with this the requirement to learn to work with others, and you get the kind of group problem solving, discovery learning, project-based approach of so many schools, courses, and training centers. The case study of law schools and management courses is the most frequent vehicle for this type of learning, supplemented by "group-effectiveness" training embracing such devices as T-groups, power and influence workshops, and team-building laboratories, all admirable in their own cultures.

Athenian cultures tend to think of people as resourceful humans rather than human resources, regarding them as people who are responsible for their own ultimate destinies but who at the moment are available for assignment to particular problem areas. In these cultures, therefore, there is more likely to be a bidding system for jobs and positions than there is in the Apollonian steady-state. Leaders recruit teams, or individuals apply to join groups. Assignment is usually subject to the agreement of both individual and leader. A commando unit in which the commander has had no say in the choice of his men will not be very effective. If there are appraisal and development schemes in these cultures, they are likely to be so devised that the *individual* initiates any discussion or action. Self-development is encouraged, and mobility among organizations is not frowned upon.

Ways of Influencing and Changing

Organizational Athenians bow down to wisdom and expertise. To command in a task culture, you must have earned the respect of those you command. This command can then be exercised through the socially acceptable form of *persuasion*. Obedience is replaced by agreement. There is a lot of talk, argument, and discussion in task cultures, in which discussion documents abound and it is expected that what is written is read. In this culture, unlike those of Zeus and Apollo, you begin to rely on the rational strength of your case to win your way. To do so, however, it is first necessary to define the problem and win agreement to that definition and to its priority for the group. "Problem solving," say Athenians, "starts with problem finding."

Task cultures work best when a heterogenous group of talents finds its homogeneity through identification with a common cause, task, or problem. The first step to influence in these cultures, then, is to change the definition of the focal problem or task. Change the problem and you change the direction of activity. Only in cases of imminent disaster can the new problem be imposed. More usually it grows out of a changed consensus in the group. Any newcomer wishing to change things must first remember that he cannot even begin to address the critical problem until he has the respect of the group. But this respectability can be imported; that is, it can be earned in one place and transported to another. Athenians are cosmopolitans to a degree, believing that expertise travels and that one is a citizen of the world, not of one organization.

The task culture is beloved by the "new" professionals (the marketing, production, planning, and development experts of modern corporations) because of this transferability of expertise. In a task culture you can gain the credibility of an expert without the kind of personal charisma necessary in a Zeus culture. These qualifications act as an introduction in the Athena culture, whereas you need a patron or a track record in the world of Zeus. Of course, if your subsequent actions give the lie to your qualifications, these will quickly be eroded, whereas in time a track record amounts to a qualification and can then be transported to another organization.

Athenian task cultures thus tend to deal with change by "boxing the problem." This is an organizational technique consisting of identifying the problem, allocating staff time to dealing with it, and recognizing this new distribution of resources and priorities by putting a new box on the organization chart: a box whose title is, in effect, the problem. If, for instance, the problem is one of coordinating subsidiary plans, a group (permanent or temporary) can be set up to deal with this dilemma and is legitimized by the allocation of a box on the chart and the appropriate title of division, department, unit, group, committee, or task force (depending on its size and permanence). It is usually possible to identify a task culture's concerns by examining the titles of its current committees or study groups.

A predominantly Apollonian or role culture sensibly surrounds itself with many task culture groups to attend to its needs for change. A Greek temple organization, finding itself in a changing market or technology, rapidly becomes cross-strutted with a variety of coordinating teams, planning groups, and investigating committees. This is fine. The confusion arises when such groups believe that the effectiveness of their reasoning influences the Apollonian part of the organization or when the steady-state Apollonians ignore the task groups because they are inadequately enmeshed in the formal authority structure. Problem solving, you see, is fine as a method of influence *inside* the task culture, but to influence another culture you have to play its games.

Athena into Zeus Won't Go

The top echelon of the consulting company was being reorganized. Times were leaner, and a new, tougher and more directive style of management was, probably rightly, thought to be required at the top. The four chief barons conferred privately, off site, meeting in their own homes. The large, consultative top management group was to be disbanded. Its leisurely, reflective, debating style would be too cumbersome for the new urgency they wanted to instill. Instead, these four would comprise the chairman's group, which would be the top power group in the consulting company.

Then there would be an administration committee to look after what we would call the steady-state activities. Although very necessary, this was, in this organization, very much the housekeeping role and consequently of low status.

But the consulting company had other longer-term problems: its future, for instance, and the question of standards and product quality, talent, development, and recruitment. In a typically Athenian fashion, part-time committees were set up to "deal with" these matters, and the chairmanship was given to the most appropriate people in the firm.

One of them refused the task—to the amazement of the chairman (after all, the appointment was by way of being a compliment). "You do not understand the nature of power in this organization," explained the refusing manager. "Unless the chairmen of your committees are also members of the chairman's group, their work will be ineffectual and I do not want to be busy being ineffectual."

The chairman was puzzled, angry, and hurt. A proper Athenian by nature, he saw the other's response as a greedy and irresponsible bid for personal status. The manager, probably rightly, saw a Zeus culture forming at the top of a rather fuzzy and extravagant task culture, a Zeus culture in which membership of the club would be an essential prerequisite to the exercise of influence at the top. Talking from different, but undeclared, cultural assumptions, the argument degenerated into a personal quarrel.

The committees exist. They do not matter very much—Athenian appendages to the new Zeus club. The chairman is contemplating joining them, "to beef them up a bit." The manager, like Achilles, sulks in his tent. A cultural misunderstanding clutters up the organization.

Ways of Motivating and Rewarding

Athenians like variety and become bored by certainty. But they are problem solvers rather than difference makers, looking for a dilemma rather than a vacuum. In this way they differ from Zeus. Just as in the myth Athena sprang fully armed from the head of Zeus, so in a way, the Athenian culture can provide the brains for Zeus's impulse. Athenians, however, also respect expertise and professionalism and therefore are concerned with their own self-advancement, self-advancement in a professional rather than hierarchical sense, although promotion can often be the outward sign of professional success.

When Athenians talk about "getting the job done," they bring a different flavor to the phrase than when Apollonians say it. Athenians imply a problem solved and dealt with—something finished once for all—whereas Apollonians work in a continuous present and might more commonly say "getting on with the job." Thus it is that an Athenian prefers the task to be defined rather than the role, for he wishes to keep discretion over the means to any given end. "Objectives" he will buy, not "role descriptions." Teams—the personalities and talents who make them up— interest him greatly, whereas the Apollonian prefers to know the rules governing their interaction. The Athenian is content to be judged by results, whereas in Apollo cultures the results can seldom be attributed to any individual or set of individuals, and so it must be means, the performance in a role, that must be judged.

Athenians therefore flourish under conditions of variety, problem solving, and opportunity for self-development. They respond to payment by results, to group assignments, and to "defined uncertainty"—the solution of identified challenges. Appropriately, they work in the development areas of organizations, in predominantly task cultures, such as consultancies, research groups, advertising agencies, or, increasingly, at the very top of very large organizations. They become restless in the steady-state and can be indecisive in crises.

Money or . . . ?

Lisl Klein tells of an experience that illustrates the difficulty of pinning down the precise nature of motivation.[3]

A maintenance mechanic in a chemical process firm was being interviewed. It was an unstructured interview, during which he talked freely for two hours about his job. At first he took a fairly instrumental line: "All I'm interested in is the money. This firm pays well, and that's the only reason I have come here. What a working man wants from his job is his paycheck, and don't let anybody kid you about other fancy notions."

Half an hour later he was talking about the firm and

discussing various things that he thought were wrong with it. The interviewer said nothing, but the mechanic seemed to think he was being inconsistent, because he stopped himself. Then he said, "Well, you see, when you get a bit older and the kids are off your hands and you've paid for the house and your wife's got a washing machine, you don't need money so much any more. You find you start noticing the firm. And by God, it can annoy you!" (Some Athena urges?)

Half an hour after that, he remarked, "You know— what I really like is when the machine goes wrong and *I'm* the one who knows how to put it right." (Zeus in a crisis?)

(Klein comments that any definition of his motivation would depend on where the interview finished).

The Existential Culture (Dionysus)

Dionysians, of course, are very different again. It is anathema to a Dionysian to be classified except as *not* belonging to another classification! They like to be individuals, exceptions to all generalizations. It is therefore very difficult, and perhaps mistaken, to describe them as a class. Nevertheless, the growth of individualism in organizations is becoming one of the central dilemmas of society, and I have defined it as such in this book, so the difficult must be attempted.

Ways of Thinking and Learning

Dionysians, for example, defy rigid classification in their thinking habits. These depend a bit on their chosen profession: Scientists may well think like Apollonians, artists like Zeus. To be a Dionysian, however, is to think—whether or not it is true—that you have nothing much to learn from anyone. Only from life. For those at the top of their profession, this may well be true in fact as well as in perception. In others, less eminent or less skilled, it can seem like unfounded arrogance, disrespect, or, at times in youth, downright rudeness.

Dionysians therefore prefer to learn by immersion, by new

experiences. It often happens that a Dionysian gives up a job or a post or a project when he is the total master of it, just because he is the total master of it and therefore has nothing left to learn. It is a habit infuriating to employers and clients alike.

Dionysian Masochism?

André Previn, a conductor, was being interviewed on the radio. "Why," asked the interviewer, "did you leave Hollywood and the composing of musical scores for the films just when you were doing so well and had that world at your feet?" "Because," said Previn, "I began to wake up in the morning without any pain in my stomach. I was no longer unsure of my capabilities."

A publisher observed, "Academic authors are always bored by the books we want them to write, which build on their established reputation, whereas publishers are always worried by the books academics want to write, which are about fields and topics new to them."

"What I hate about careers," said the young arts graduate, "is that you know what's going to happen to you. It's so boring. It's the unexpected that develops you, swimming out of your depth."

Dionysians resent any attempt by others, particularly an organization, to plan their futures or develop their abilities. They want opportunities but demand the right to choose among them. They talk of sabbaticals, of second or third careers, of dropping out or dropping in. In one or two organizations, the notion of "educational credits" has been established as a way of meeting the developmental needs of Dionysians. Educational credits are, like paid holidays, made a legal entitlement of the individual. A credit is one week's leave plus expenses for development purposes (usually a "course"). An individual may qualify for two credits per year, which can be accumulated for up to five years. He can spend his credits any time, subject to the agreement of his superior on the exact dates and on the "developmental" character of his proposed activity. In this way, opportunity is provided by the organization, but the choice and final decision are the individual's.

Ways of Influencing and Changing

It is hard to influence Dionysians. Since they do not acknowledge the power of the organization or see themselves as working *for* the organization (as opposed to *in* it), there are no organizational weapons to use against them. Dionysians respect only people, but there is no predicting what they will respect them for. It can be for their talent or for their faces. Or it may be talent one month and personality the next.

It is this very unpredictability that gives them the personal freedom essential to the culture. Even the words *influence* or *change* smack of an infringement of liberty to a Dionysian. It follows that any attempt to influence or change a Dionysian will be a much more contracted procedure than in the other cultures, although in a sense any process of change or influence involves some notion of "exchange," in which one person or persons do or get something in recognition of something else.

A Dionysian negotiation always starts with the stated or implied opener, "What will induce you to . . . ?" Only from an intimate knowledge of the person involved can one begin to make predictions as to what the particular inducement will be. As in all Dionysian situations, everything is particular—peculiar to the time, place, and person, not general. Dionysians are therefore very difficult people to "manage." To anyone used to working on broad assumptions of similarity among similar people, it is very confusing to find that what works with A does not produce the same results with B, who is apparently a doctor, architect, activist, or professor in exactly the same situation.

Of course, we all have Dionysian streaks in us, but most people confine these to certain portions of their life—their gardens, their social life, their holidays. To carry them into organizations of work can make it very difficult for those in charge, for the endless series of individual negotiations necessary to make life both unpredictable and exhausting. It is for this reason that Dionysians have to put on the cloak of another culture or to make themselves irreplaceable if they are not eventually to be evicted or discarded by their employer.

Dionysian organizations (partnerships, usually) are therefore managed in a one-on-one fashion. The "leader" interacts with each individually, meetings being called only disseminate information or to ask for ideas on a situation of common interest.

Ways of Motivating and Rewarding

In the areas of motivation and reward, Dionysians are, of course, the most individualistic of the lot. Once again, they are hard to characterize as a generality precisely because they insist on—almost exaggerate—their individuality. Like Zeus characters, they want personally to make a difference to the world, but it does not have to be through power or people or resources. It does not even have to be noticed. A poem in a corner, a picture unseen, a patient healed unnoticed, can also be reward enough to Dionysians. It is interesting that the true Dionysian professions actually forbid any form of advertising, whereas the more Athenian professions (consultants, estate agents, architects) find more of less discreet ways to promote their fame.

Dionysians value personal freedom above all, freedom to act and speak as they wish, but particularly freedom of their time. Obligation to a community or organization they recognize as a necessary part of the social contract, but they will, without rancor, try to incur as little of it as possible in return for their own rights. They like to be consulted, with a reserve right of veto, but not to participate; to be asked for their views, but not obliged to give them.

If this seems an essentially selfish view of the psychological contract, one must remember that these people do not really want to work in organizations at all. They are loners who gather in organizations or communities or partnerships purely for convenience, their convenience. As part of a larger and more culture-mixed organization, these Dionysian values, or psychological contracts, can be tolerated only if the individuals have great personal talent, if they are full professionals. As we shall see, the problems arise when the untalented begin to demand Dionysian contracts.

The first essential, then, of organizational efficiency is cultural purity. To each his own god. Harmony is health. It is when the gods compete within one activity that confusion results, for then the law of cultural propriety is violated.

If harmony is health, the healthy (happy) organization is one that uses the appropriate methods and assumptions of influence in a particular culture. Thus persuasion, logical reasoning (Athenian), is effective in a Zeus culture only if it comes from a member of the club and, in an Apollo structure, only if accompanied by the requisite authority. Techniques and rule books (Apollonian) are ignored by Zeus figures unless it suits their purpose to use them or they respect the author (if he can be identified). Changing people around has little impact on an Apollonian organization, although it can be a major learning experience for the individual. Hence "job rotation" is a favored form of individual development in Apollonian organizations, as it develops the individual while leaving the organization untouched. Conversely, changing the structure or the procedures (Apollonian) has little effect on Zeus organizations if the key people, the club, remain the same. In these organizations, structural change is often only a means to changing key people without too much trauma.

My descriptions of the motivational contract are, of course, stereotypes. As I have already pointed out, we are none of us, individuals or organizations, culturally pure. All of us like a little predictability in our lives as well as a little variety. All of us want at some time to make a personal impact. But if we are honest with ourselves (and who has more incentive to be?), we can admit that the proportions of the cultural mix differ in each of us. And there lies the problem of motivation. There is no one answer, no universal panacea to be found in piecework systems, in job security, in lowered taxation, in job satisfaction.

Harmony, as always, is health. Reward systems designed for Apollonian role cultures, linking role performance to hierarchical promotion, will not be effective if the psychological contracts operating are those of a Zeus culture. Apollonians understand deferred gratification—they can wait a longer time for their ultimate glory. But Zeus and Athena people want quick results and rewards, discounting the future at a high rate, living for today or tomorrow rather than the year, or the decade, after next.

Discretionary Differences?

Elliott Jaques suggested that individuals differ in their innate capacity for discretion.[4] He measures discretion by the maximum time that the individual can operate without a review of the quality of his performance. Simple tasks usually have a short "time span of discretion," maybe even hours, whereas senior management roles have discretion spans measured in years.

Several studies point to a consistent number of strata of discretion spans in organizational roles, as follows:

Time Span	Stratum
(?) 20 yrs	7
10 yrs	6
5 yrs	5
2 yrs	4
1 yr	3
Less than 1 yr	2
Less than 3 months	1

Giving people work that requires more discretion than their current capacity is very stressful. Jaques argues that in large organizations, most jobs are at the fifth, sixth, and even seventh strata but that there are few people around with those capacities.

It is intriguing to speculate whether the cultures, and cultural types, differ in the levels of strata involved. Maybe Zeus cultures operate with short time horizons and levels of 4 and below? If so, such individuals would find the top of large organizations very stressful places. Athenians, too, may not feel comfortable with time spans longer than two years. And Dionysians? And some Apollonians?

We don't know, but Jaques's research may be yet another reason to explain why cultures don't mix.

The confusion between Zeus and Dionysus is a very real one. Both act as individuals in situations that, whether real or imagined, demand their personal intervention. The difference lies in the power behind their action. Zeus relies on his control over vital resources and the force of his character, or charisma, backed by his experience and record of success. Dionysians are accepted because of their professional competence, because they are unique craftsmen whose skills cannot easily be replicated. A bad Zeus can make things happen, albeit in the wrong way. A bad Dionysus is ignored. A Zeus can be incompetent in the eyes of others and still function. A Dionysus depends on the respect of others to have any impact. On the other hand, nature is fair. Zeus needs power and wants impact. Dionysus often does not care. "Take it or leave it" is not a Zeus remark, but it could be a Dionysian one. Dionysians are more self-contained, inner directed, and concerned about their craft. A Zeus without people to interact with will die, and the entrepreneur who claims that he will retire to his orchard when he has made his pile, is usually lying: His need to intervene in the affairs of others will not be satisfied with apple trees. The Dionysian, on the other hand, can be happy cultivating a garden visited only by himself. Yet because both Zeus and Dionysus characters intervene personally, relying on their personal prowess, it is often hard to distinguish them by their behavior. The dedicated scientist, intent on an idea, can be just as dominant, even ruthless, as the Victorian mill owner. Many Zeus people define themselves as organizational craftsmen, enthusiastic professionals, and are both surprised and hurt by accusations of dictatorship.

Formal documented schemes of management by objectives turn into time-consuming rituals in Athenian cultures, which find their own ways of defining the common purposes of their groups. To apply the "group-effectiveness" training of the Athenian culture to the steady-state is only to foster insecurity and uncertainty or, in Zeus cultures, outright rebellion. The notion of patron and protégé is anathema to Apollonian cultures, which regard crown princes as disruptive to their grading schemes. Yet in their proper place, these devices work. You cannot run a factory like a trading company, or a trading company like a consultancy. So the habits of thought and of learning are just as unlikely to be identical. They are, in fact, very different and need to be seen to be such. Cultural propriety must be preserved.

The Missing Garbage Bags

In one community, it was the practice to collect garbage in plastic bags, which were distributed to householders for this purpose by the drivers of the garbage trucks.

These plastic bags had a value on the open market, as some of the truck drivers apparently discovered. At least, it soon became clear that many of the new bags were not reaching the householders for whom they were intended.

It was, therefore, decided to set up a separate unit, with its own vans, to distribute these bags independently of the garbage vehicles.

Now truck drivers are a special breed. Their cab is their kingdom, the road their territory. Once on the road, they answer to no man. They are the Dionysians of the motorways or the Zeuses of the delivery services. In their own spheres, they wield dictatorial power, as any housewife who offends a delivery driver knows. Garbage collectors are no exception. They are individuals with their own freedoms. Leash them if you can, and dare.

Private marketeering can be one of the side attractions of this minibuccaneering. This is often more a game than a crime, and losing is getting caught. To stop the game as a penalty for catching some losers is seen as unjust, even—perversely perhaps—as an infringement on their liberty. Zeus is humiliated; Dionysus is snubbed. Their interventionist energies, their wish and ability to be noticed, will now be turned inward on the system instead of outward. Their power will be negative.

In this case, the local authority sought to reduce the number of drivers, to compensate for manning the vans. The drivers retaliated by working to rule and threatening a strike. The action of the authority brought the drivers together as nothing else ever had. After this, muttering increased, and morale decreased.

Zeus will not willingly, or cheaply, submit to Apollo.

Enter Athena

The new chief executive—the radical son of his more traditional founding father—was eager to put more life and humanity into his father's viable but unspectacular dye-manufacturing company. This company employed 150 people and produced a range of dyes from base stocks for a number of long-standing customers. Their methods, of both manufacture and accounting, were old-fashioned but reliable, and adequate in a world in which things did not change very much, growth was slow but steady, and the labor turnover was under 5 percent.

"Groups," the son announced, "were the way to work: groups in which we earned respect from our colleagues by an honest sharing of both problems and perceptions, in which the pursuit of a common goal by equals would produce a new synergy."

Although most of the managers and supervisors did not even understand the words he was using, he did after all pay them, so they reluctantly agreed to attend a weekend "group dynamics workshop" to find out about these new ways of working. A group dynamics workshop is a T-group, a method designed to help people explore the way that groups work and how they can work in them, by a mix of discussion, exchange of perceptions, small tasks, and shared reflections.

By Saturday night, Bill had revealed his true feelings about Fred, who was unlikely to forget them in a hurry; the chief executive found that the group had discovered at least one common enemy—himself; Tom, the accountant, had withdrawn behind a wall of silence; and overall, a new sense of unease and defensiveness had entered the usual bantering conversation of the group.

The young chief executive was puzzled. It had worked so well at college and in that consulting group he had been attached to for a while. What had gone wrong?

Athenian ways do not fit the more staid and formal roles and ways of an Apollo organization, which, like it or not, was what he had inherited.

The questionnaire at the end of this chapter provides one way of analyzing and codifying the cultural preferences of your organization and yourself. Questionnaires, of course, are fallible, particularly when one fills them in for oneself about oneself. Add to that the fact that organizations are not hard objective realities, like chairs, which can be objectively measured and described, or is your character or personality (in spite of the attempts of some psychologists to define them). So it is clear that the scores that you arrive at can be only your view, from where you stand at this point in time, of the organization and yourself.

The interesting thing would be to give the questionnaire to a variety of people and then to compare their ideas of the organization (and of you?) with yours. A lot would depend on where they worked in the organization, whether they were looking up or down or across it when they filled in the questionnaire, and how satisfied they were in their own lives. To some extent, they probably change their cultural behavior as they do different parts of their job. And so they should.

Questionnaire on the Cultures of Organizations[5]

To complete the questionnaire, proceed as follows:

1. Consider the organization you work for, as a whole. What sets of values, what beliefs, what forms of behavior could be said to be typical of it? Look at the four statements under each of the nine headings in the questionnaire. Under each heading, rank the four statements in order of "best fit" to the organization as you see it (i.e., put "1" by the statement that best represents the organization, "2" by the next best, and so on). Put the figures in the column under Organization.

2. When you have done this for the organization, then go through the whole process again, this time for yourself, reflecting your own preferences and beliefs. Try not to look at your rankings under Organization while you do this, so that your second ranking will be truly independent.

When you have ranked all the statements under each of the two columns, add up the scores for all the statements marked (a) under each heading, then the scores for all the statements listed (b), and so on (e.g., a total score of 9 for all the [b] statements would mean that you had ranked the [b] statement "1" in each of the nine headings).

You should now be able to complete the following table:

	All (a) Statements	All (b) Statements	All (c) Statements	All (d) Statements	Total
The whole organization					90
You					90

As in most questionnaires, you will want to qualify all your answers with the remark "It all depends. . . ." You will find it hard in some instances to find any great difference, in your own mind, among some of the statements. Do not let this deter you. The questionnaire results will not be precisely accurate, but they should provide useful indications. You will find that the best way to proceed when trying to rank each set of statements is to trust your first, almost intuitive reactions. Do not linger over them too long.

When you have completed the questionnaire and added up the scores, turn to page 68 for an explanation of the total scores.

QUESTIONNAIRE

Self   Organization

1

(a)   *A good boss*

Is strong, decisive, and firm but fair. He or she is protective, generous, and indulgent to loyal subordinates.

_____   _____

(b) Is impersonal and correct, avoiding the exercise of authority for his or her own advantage. He or she demands from subordinates only what is required by the formal system.

_____   _____

(c) Is egalitarian and influential in matters concerning the task. He or she uses authority to obtain the resources needed to do the job.

_____   _____

(d) Is concerned and responsive to the personal needs and values of others and provides satisfying and growth-stimulating work opportunities for subordinates.

_____   _____

Self		Organization
2	*A good subordinate*	
(a)	Is hardworking, loyal to the interests of his or her superior, resourceful, and _____ trustworthy.	_____
(b)	Is responsible and reliable, meeting the duties and responsibilities of the job and avoiding actions that would surprise or _____ embarrass his or her superior.	_____
(c)	Is self-motivated to contribute his or her best to the task and is open with ideas and suggestions. Is nevertheless willing to give the lead to others when they show _____ greater expertise or ability.	_____
(d)	Is vitally interested in the development of his or her own potentialities and is open to learning and receiving help. Also respects the needs and values of others and is willing to give help and contribute to _____ their development.	_____

Self		Organization
3	*A good member of the organization gives first priority to*	
(a)	_____ The personal demands of the boss.	_____
(b)	The duties, responsibilities, and requirements on his or her own role and the cus- _____ tomary standards of personal behavior.	_____
(c)	The requirements of the task for skill, _____ ability, energy, and material resources.	_____
(d)	The personal needs of the individuals in- _____ volved.	_____

Self		Organization
4	*People who do well in the organization*	
(a)	Are politically aware, like taking risks _____ and operating on their own.	_____
(b)	Are conscientious and responsible, with a strong sense of loyalty to the organiza- _____ tion.	_____
(c)	Are technically competent and effective, with a strong commitment to getting the _____ job done.	_____

Self   Organization

(d)   Are effective and competent in personal
            relationships, with a strong commitment
            to the growth and development of indi-
_____   vidual talents.   _____

Self   Organization
5   *The organization treats the individual*
(a)   As a trusted agent whose time and en-
            ergy are at the disposal of those who run
_____   the organization.   _____
(b)   As though his or her time and energy
            were available through a contract, having
_____   rights and responsibilities on both sides.   _____
(c)   As a co-worker who has committed his or
            her skills and abilities to the common
_____   cause.   _____
(d)   As an interesting and talented person in
_____   his or her own right.   _____

Self   Organization
6   *People are controlled and influenced by*
(a)   The personal exercise of rewards, punish-
_____   ments, or charisma.   _____
(b)   The impersonal exercise of economic
            and political power to enforce proce-
_____   dures and standards of performance.   _____
(c)   The communication and discussion of
            task requirements leading to appropriate
            action motivated by a personal commit-
_____   ment to achieve goals.   _____
(d)   An intrinsic interest and enjoyment in
            the activities to be done, and/or concern
            and caring for the needs of the other peo-
_____   ple involved.   _____

Self   Organization
7   *It is legitimate for one person to control an-*
            other's activities
(a)   If he or she has more power and influ-
_____   ence in the organization.   _____
(b)   If his or her role prescribes that he or she
_____   is responsible for directing the other.   _____

Self			Organization
(c)	_____	If he or she has more knowledge relevant to the task at hand.	_____
(d)	_____	If he or she is accepted by those that he or she controls.	_____

Self			Organization
8		*The basis of task assignment is*	
(a)	_____	The personal needs and judgment of those who run the place.	_____
(b)	_____	The formal divisions of functions and responsibility in the system.	_____
(c)	_____	The resource and expertise requirements of the job to be done.	_____
(d)	_____	The personal wishes and needs for learning and growth of the individual organization members.	_____

Self			Organization
9		*Competition*	
(a)	_____	Is for personal power and advantages.	_____
(b)	_____	Is for a high-status position in the formal system.	_____
(c)	_____	Is for excellence of contribution to the task.	_____
(d)	_____	Is for attention to one's own personal needs.	_____

Interpretation of Questionnaire Scores

The (a) statements represent a Zeus "club" culture; the (b) statements represent the Apollo "role" culture; the (c) statements represent the Athenian "task" culture; and the (d) statements represent the Dionysian "existential" culture. The *lower* the total score is for any set of statements, the *more prevalent* that culture is in your organization or in you. A score of 9 for the (a) statements (the lowest possible total) would mean a totally pure Zeus culture. You are unlikely to have any totals as low as that.

A table that reads, for example,

	(a)	(b)	(c)	(d)	Total
Whole organization	14	12	27	37	90
You	29	24	16	21	90

would mean that your organization was a mix of Apollo and Zeus and that you prefer to be Athena backed up by Dionysus.

3

The Gods
in Balance

It is now necessary to look a little more closely at the forces that
influence the balance of gods or cultures in any organization, at
the problems of changing the mix of cultures when necessary,
and at the way of holding that balance without contaminating
the individual cultures. If the mix is wrong, or is badly balanced,
or is not changed when change is needed, the result will be a
phenomenon called *slack* or ineffectiveness, the lurking cancer
of organizations.

Effective organizations have usually formed their own balanced mix by means of experiment and continual adaptation.
They have achieved cultural propriety and minimized slack.
But if it is to continue, success must be understood. History,
the story of how it happened, is an inadequate explanation for
others to use, for history cannot be relied on to repeat itself.
I shall therefore attempt to explain, functionally rather than
historically, how effective organizations achieve the proper
balance of gods. The organized society needs more cultural
propriety in its organizations, and it needs it now; it cannot
wait for some Darwinian process of evolution to reach it in
the end.

We shall look in turn at the forces that influence the choice of
mix and the ways of changing and of managing that mix.

First: Balance Your Gods

How Do You Explain Yourself?

An American visitor to Europe commented that every time he asked the reason for something, he received the historical explanation: "Because the king met with his nobles in this way," or "Because my grandfather liked to see the mill from his bedroom," or "Because my family did not approve of schools," or "Because originally they got free travel when this firm was owned by the railway."

"In my country," said the American, "I normally get a functional explanation. Perhaps that's why you all are so interesting, and we are more efficient."

The Influencing Forces

Organizations have to live with the pressure of several countervailing forces. *Management* is the act of reconciling these forces in some blend of jobs and cultures. There can be no universal formula, for the pressures are felt differently by each organization. The best way to express these forces is to describe their effects as tendencies: "The greater the force, the more likely. . . . The principal forces are size, life cycles, work patterns, and people. After we describe their effects briefly, we will return to a discussion of what one can do about them.

Size

How many people can you relate to as individuals at any one time? Fifty? One hundred? One thousand? It all depends on how well you want to relate to them, of course, but for most people the answer must be nearer fifty than one thousand. All the cultures, except the role culture (Apollo), depend on the people in a work group knowing one another. Knowing one another implies an awareness of personality, talents, and skills, as well as just a name.

The Bigger You Are, the More Like Apollo You Will Be

That is the general tendency. My own inclination is to follow
Antony Jay's empirical rule of ten as the break point. Once you
have more than ten people in a group, ten groups in a division,
or ten divisions in a company, you must rely on formal methods
of control and coordination. The farmer with his free farm-
hands has no need of the Apollonian devices of managerial
textbooks. It all can be done intuitively and personally. The
small primary school can run perfectly well with a minimum of
impersonal coordination, hierarchies, and forms. Not so the
large secondary school. Small is non-Apollonian, which is not
the same as saying that it is beautiful, but many small companies have growth as their goal, achieve it, and hate the changes
it brings. From Zeus or Athena to Apollo is quite a violent
transition. Parkinson's law, that the administrative component
always grows faster than the rest, ignores the influence of other
factors that we have yet to examine, but if translated and downgraded from a law to a tendency, it does emphasize that increasing size means an increasing proportion of the steady-state, a
larger square.

Research and Size

As does much descriptive research on organizations, the
conclusions of research on the effects of increasing size
cause little surprise:[1]

• As the size of the organization increases, so does the
need for coordination and supervision.
• As coordination and supervision increase, so does
the bureaucracy.
• As bureaucracy increases, so do impersonal controls.
• Impersonal controls are accompanied by increases
in absenteeism and staff turnover.
• The larger the organization is, the smaller the average amount of communication among its members will
be.
• As size increases, so does specialization.
• As specialization increases, each job becomes less
complex.

• It is *not* always true (in spite of Parkinson's law) that the administrative component increases faster than the rest do.
• Apollo thrives on size.

Life Cycles

Life cycle is another term for the old chestnut of management, *rate of change*. The tendency can also be expressed as "The higher the rate of change, the larger the influence of Athena."

The difficulty is that it is very hard to assess the rate of change. As overall measures of societal tendencies, it may be appropriate to use indicators such as speed of travel or quantities of data processed. But these are of little value to an individual organization, to which it is more useful to think in terms of life cycles—products, technologies, systems. How many years will each last? When the solutions of the fathers were good enough for the sons—a generational life cycle—the Athena component in organizations was very small. At the other extreme, when the useful life of any idea is shorter than the time it took to create it (as in some very new technologies), the Athena influence is huge.

The idea of life cycles, too, should not be confined to industrial or commercial products. Diplomatic rules, educational policies, housing plans, and coordination systems all have their life cycles. When you get to minimum life cycles—only one of anything is ever made (in consulting firms, some architects' offices, art studios, and the like)—there is an almost pure Athenian culture, with the Apollonian methods reserved for the housekeeping duties of the "services and administration."

It is impossible to quantify the proportions in general terms. It would be nice to be able to state that if the life cycle equals the creative cycle, Apollo will equal Athena; if double, then double Apollo. Life is not that simple, but such a rule will do for a start, as a quantification of this tendency alone. Remember, however, that other factors are at work to influence the final mix.

In practical terms, this tendency means that organizations adapt to shortening life cycles by, for instance, (1) pulling people out of straight production into production development, or from sales to market development; (2) setting up task forces or study groups; (3) calling in consultants; (4) cutting down the production or administrative component, leaving development groups intact; and (5) creating a top management group, removed from operational responsibility. In all these cases the problem-solving capacity (Athena) is increased, not the administrative capacity (Apollo).

Work Patterns

There are three different ways to arrange the work to be done in an organization: (1) as *flows* (in which one section's work is the input for the rest), (2) as *copies* (in which the work of each section is identical), or (3) as *units* (in which the work of each section is independent).

An assembly line is the most familiar example of a *flow pattern*. It is a logical way of organizing complex, repetitive work, allowing specialization and economies of scale at each stage. A chemical process plant is an automated flow pattern. A local government office is often a clerical flow pattern, as a particular piece of paper goes through successive official stages in the office. A school or a hospital can also be regarded as a flow pattern, with students or patients as the pieces.

Branch banking, multiple stores, and gasoline stations are familiar examples of *copy patterns*. Economies of scale and coordination depend on each unit's being a replica of the others. If airline tickets were not filled in identically by every ticket agency, it would be much more difficult to arrange interchanges among airlines or communal booking facilities. If every outlet of a multiple store did its own purchasing and had its own billing procedure, the economics of mass purchasing and centralized accounting would be impossible.

Unit patterns apply where standardization is impossible or unnecessary. Trading and dealing activities, craftsman manufacture (pottery, painting, or architecture), the self-employed, and small organizations, such as farms or independent shops, all are familiar examples of this pattern.

The tendency is for flow and copy patterns to require Apollonian (role culture) methods.

Unit patterns can be Zeus-like (most frequently), Athenian (if the collaborative work of a group is needed), or Dionysian (as with most professionals). Teachers, for instance, are Dionysian in their own approach and prefer to operate as single units, yet they often find themselves part of a flow or copy organization. Dilemma!

It is not, however, only the economics of standardization that drive organizations toward flow or copy patterns. The concept of *control* is also at work. Control is important if you need to regulate or inspect quality *before* the event. It is very hard to do this systematically or efficiently in unit patterns, because quality control in unit patterns is a postfactum feature. If you make a bad deal or a bad picture or sell the wrong item in your store, the mistake will not be discovered until *after* the event. In many businesses and offices, this is not critical. Although errors are always undesirable, it is often impossible and unnecessary to avoid them altogether. We can and do learn by them. But some errors are too critical to be left for postfactum discovery. This particularly includes errors that might cost human lives, and in such cases antecedent checking is usually required by law (e.g., in aircraft manufacture, the drug industry, house building, and food manufacture). Even when it is not a legal requirement, an organization can decide that the financial cost of an error is punitive and that it must be stopped before it happens. It will then find itself insisting on copy or flow patterns of work and on an increase in the role culture (Apollo).

The takeover of a small firm by a larger one can often result in the unit pattern of the small firm changing to conform to the copy pattern of the larger one. This causes a culture change, usually from Zeus to Apollo. Once again, the culture shock to the individuals can be severe, the more so because it is not understood.

From Unit to Copy, or Zeus to Apollo

In the lumber yard, the old man was sawing my length of lumber for me with quite unnecessary care and precision.

"You look as if you love that wood," I said. "Were you ever a professional carpenter?"

"Yes, indeed," he replied. "I used to work for X" (naming a famous furniture designer).

"Why did you leave to come to a lumber yard, then?"

"Well, X got taken over by YZ company (a conglomerate with a furniture division), and everything had to be made to fit their standard designs. Suddenly, it wasn't fun any more. All the pride went out of the work. And then they said they didn't need so many people, so the older craftsmen went—the more expensive ones, you see. In the old days, Terence (the owner and founder) used to be around—we all knew him and knew how he wanted things—great man. After "they" came, it was all forms and regulations and inspectors. Not the same at all. So now I just work to get money. It's OK here. Just a job."

People

Much as one may sometimes deplore it in others, people are different! This is not going to be an excursion into personality theory—that is an unnecessarily complex field for our cultural preferences. But there is probably a bit of each god in each of us, and we all are to some degree adaptable; that is, when we have to, we can live in alien cultures, though usually unwillingly and at a price.

Our cultural preferences are probably thrust on us by our early experiences and environments. No doubt some of us are born as Zeus or Dionysus, but since these cultures describe the ways that we relate to our fellow men, it is likely that our attitudes toward them are due more to our environments than to our genes. There is good evidence to suggest that certain cultures are more popular in certain societies, indicating that there is some kind of societal conditioning.

Japanese are different from Italians, aren't they? But were they *born* different in their cultural preferences? Our education can bend us toward cultures or away from them, as can the values and customs of our early homes. Father's occupation is still the best predictor of the son's choice of job, and probably of culture as well.

And although people certainly can adapt, they do not necessarily adapt easily. If your organization is currently manned by Apollonians, wanting a secure life and a fair day's pay for a fair day's work, it will be hard to create a range of developmental cells and Athenian attitudes. You must work with what you've got in the way of people. That applies to the organization, to the catchment area of your work, and to society as a whole. Deportation is becoming as rare in organizations as in society (it is almost necessary to prove an illegal offense before dismissing someone), and a wholesale restocking of an organization is unthinkable in democratic societies.

The tendencies of the "people forces" are too varied to be easily summarized. Some of them are obvious:

Youth does not relish Apollo, with that culture's need to play down individuality.

The more you've been educated formally, the further down the scale of cultures you are likely to be (e.g., doctors and architects, with unusually long training periods, are often Dionysian; the illiterate driver or entrepreneur, a Zeus).

Educational philosophies that emphasize the individual and his development (as opposed to the inculcation of received wisdom or values), produce people with Athenian or Dionysian preferences.

The hungry obey, and the contented argue. Apollo cultures rely on an economic contract between organization and employee, a contract that works best where economics matter most.

Personality characteristics affect cultural preferences. A restless intuitive extrovert finds Apollo tiresome. Individualists dislike Athena, with her group emphasis, as much as they do Apollo. Conformists prefer Apollo.

And so on.

Remember that these are tendencies, not laws. As humans we have the delightful ability to be the exceptions to our own generalizations.

Do the Gods Have Personalities?

In his popular book *Know Your Own Personality*,[2] Eysenck related two of the personality dimensions that he uses to categorize personality (introversion–extraversion and stable–unstable) with the traditional divisions of the ancients. It is interesting to speculate (there is no factual evidence) whether the quadrants provide clues to the personalities that I have associated with the different gods. Dionysus is the difficult one to fit into the picture. A law unto himself, a Dionysian can perhaps be found in any quadrant, although some of the characteristics of the "empty" quadrant (Melancholic) must fit many a "loner" (see diagram on p. 80).

The Choice of Blend

Where do we go from here? The organization is a mix of four activities (steady-state, development, asterisk, and management), each with its cultural god or gods. The proportion of each activity is influenced by the four forces. Thus a large organization with long life cycles, operating in a low-technology facsimile pattern with minimally educated workers from a depressed area, is very likely—almost certainly, in fact—to have evolved with a large number of steady-state activities and to be dominated by an Apollo role culture. Examples are some canning factories, perhaps; the automobile industry, in some of its parts; "nuts and bolts" manufacturers of any size; and the textile industry of yesterday.

A small organization, with highly trained craftsmen making objects to order on a unit basis, resembles a Dionysian partnership. The account teams of an advertising agency, smaller, with short life cycles and requiring talented groups of people, will be very Athenian if successful, although some agencies have been built up by the careful selection of a few Zeus characters with their own webs (miniagencies, in fact, under one umbrella).

If you want to know how you arrived where you are, this method of cultural analysis will explain it. If you want to know why there are more creaks and groans in the organization than you would choose, this may provide the clue (a culture mix out of line with the principal forces). If you individually are unfulfilled or uninspired or underpaid, this analysis may show you why (an Athenian trapped in a temple?). More generally, cul-

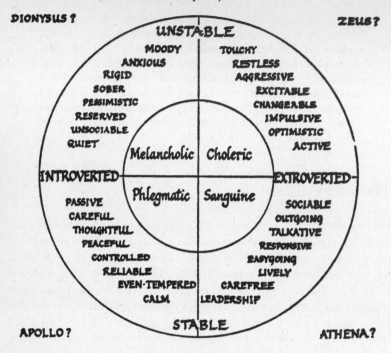

tural analysis indicates the underlying reason for much of the incompetence in our organized society.

Work Types and People Types

Is your work pattern recurrent (a repeating schedule of events) or fragmented?

Is it troubleshooting or long term, requiring sustained attention? Is it responding or self-generating?

These questions come from Rosemary Stewart's investigations of the pattern of managerial work.[3] She finds three basic patterns, and some mixed.

Pattern 1, Systems Maintenance (works manager, production manager, branch manager): Handling exceptions, responding to problems, monitoring performance. A fragmented work pattern, particularly in a variable market or work-flow situation, more crises than predictability. Frequently found in middle and junior management positions, not usually found in senior management except in small companies or with individuals who like to work in this way. Suits individuals who are energetic, resourceful, decisive, and perhaps restless. Zeus perhaps?

Pattern 2, Systems Administration (financial accounting, staff manager): Concerned with the accurate processing of information and the administration of systems. The more formalized the organization is, the more of these administrative, recurrent, time-deadline jobs there will be, particularly in the middle of junior levels. Suits those who like security and deadlines. Apollo?

Pattern 3, Project (research manager, project leader, product sales manager): Long-term tasks, often of a one-time nature. Little recurrent work, more need for sustained attention. A greater need for self-generation; any fragmentation is self-imposed. Found at all managerial levels. Suits those who can sustain a self-generating interest over a long time. Athena?

Pattern 4, Mixed (general manager, production engineer): A mixture of the previous three. The occupant of the job must vary his work pattern. Management?

Changes in the Balance

Any balance of gods and cultures, once achieved, is bound to be only temporary. Organizations must respond continually to their environment, even if they do not themselves set out to change it. Growth is one typical, self-induced problem of cultural change.

A small pottery factory of craftsmen, inspired by its success to grow and mechanize, will run into conflicts as Dionysians are confronted with Apollonian systems. The people will resent the new need to keep count and to record, to itemize and to cost. They will dislike the necessity of employing nonpotters at comparable salaries to sell or keep the accounts. They may hire an "administrator" and hope that these new features of their life will go away. They won't. Although they themselves have created these new forces, their creatures have lives, or at least cultures, of their own.

This "stage of growth" problem is a common one. Zeus begets

Apollo as the system grows. Then Athena is needed to maintain the development. *Management* comes to mean the coordination of all three, and sometimes four gods in one whole. Previously, management meant Zeus. Now it only sometimes does. Naturally, people find it hard to realize that a way of behaving that worked yesterday does not, cannot, work today. Self-imposed culture change of this sort is very stressful. It seems to carry with it a loss of identity as the culture shock is personalized—"I can no longer make things happen; what has gone wrong with *me?*"

The irony of success often lies in the fact that the methods that brought success are not those that are best suited to maintaining it. The commander who won battles is often the wrong person to administer the territories he conquered. The planners are often the wrong people to implement their plans—culturally wrong, I mean—as the saga of the Bosco Chemical Factory demonstrates.

The Bosco Chemical Saga

Bosco Chemicals U.K. Ltd. had been doing well. Its eight lines of imported pharmaceutical products had produced an annual growth of 25 percent in turnover and profits. Hitherto, it had been essentially a field sales force based in a warehouse in London, but the company decided that its turnover now justified doing the blending and formulation in a factory of its own. Based on estimated factory costs and the expectation of a continued growth in sales, the economics of the venture appeared good, for the base stock was available locally and the imported finished products had been expensive.

As it was historically only a distributing organization, Bosco had no manufacturing competence. So it bought some, the best. It hired a group of nine people to oversee the design and construction of the factory and then to be its first management team. The nine were young, highly qualified, and well paid, and among them they covered the range of competences required. They were headed by Martin, age thirty-four, the factory manager designate. Martin typified his team. He was idealistic and enthusiastic and saw this job as an opportunity to show that factory work could be meaningful and interesting as well as profitable to both individual and organization.

For two years, the nine worked together in one large

room, dominated by a model of the new factory in the center. They planned everything from the layout of the machines to the decor of the refreshment room, from pay scales to uniforms. They sat in a circle. This in itself mirrored Martin's approach to management, a collaborative problem-solving activity spurred by mutual respect among colleagues. He hoped that the whole factory of four hundred people would work like that. The room, when you visited it, was bubbling with excitement, ideas, and lively good fellowship.

In the third year the factory opened, only a month behind schedule. There was a backlog of orders, piled up in anticipation of own manufacture. But there was also a start of worldwide recession in the industry and a consequent tightening of margins. Inflation in Britain was starting to rise. The first months were difficult (teething problems, they called it), with machines breaking down, operators without experience, unanticipated quality problems. The next year was a disaster. Sales were falling, and the sales force were putting great pressure on the factory for immediate delivery, shorter production runs, special orders, and the like. But the factory was planned on the assumption of long, computer-calculated, standard production schedules. The planned system could not cope. Instead, endless interim arrangements had to be made. Day was lived by day. Costs escalated. Tempers flared. The planned room for expansion (in staff and facilities) now looked like overcapacity without the expected increase in sales. Redundancies were ordered. Unions moved in.

The "nine" met in almost constant session. In accordance with their tradition, every problem was classified as a project and assigned a project team. After six months, there were forty-seven projects, and Bert (the production engineer) was involved in twenty-three of them. Martin was losing his hair and getting divorced. There was a general feeling in the group of puzzlement, dismay, and irrational anger at fate. "How could it be going wrong? We all are talented, young, hardworking committed people. Why isn't it working?"

The company boss blamed Martin. He should get tough. Kick a few people. Shout more. Less of this end-less committee work. Martin wanted time. You can't start up a factory in under two years. Participative problem solving must be the best way. Mike (production manager) blamed participative problem solving. "It's just a pill factory," he said. "You don't need brains, only live bodies and a system." Everyone else blamed the "nine." "Why don't they do their job?" they said. "Always asking us to help with their problems. It's their business to manage, not ours. We knew there was a catch to all these fringe benefits and luxury coffee rooms."

And then they started leaving. Three of the nine left for other companies, seeing no promotional prospects in Bosco. Martin fired one after an argument (which did a lot for his self-confidence). Redundancy slimmed down the workforce. Experience began to keep the machines working. Martin was unexpectedly offered the job of new product manager in the U.S. parent company and accepted. Mike took over. Systems superseded projects. Participative problem solving was replaced in the jargon by "role and responsibility." The "nine" was now "three," reporting to Mike. There were regular monthly meetings for information exchange. Mike solved the problems and told the others.

They say it's boring, but the results look good. Athena for creating, Apollo for running a factory. But it's hard for the same men to excel in initiating and in steady-state activities. Organizations can adapt, but only with pain and time, unless they understand what's happening to them.

The general pattern is that a change of any magnitude causes a subsequent change in the balance of cultures and gods. If that cultural change does not take place, there is a mismatch between the demands of the work and the ways of managing it: Success has bred inefficiency through cultural imbalance. But cultural change of the order needed in these situations is difficult to bring about deliberately. We are creatures of cultural habits and do not change gods easily, particularly when those gods have served us well in the past. It need cause us no surprise, therefore, to find that we have to be frightened into cultural change—a kind of organizational culture shock is needed. The sequence of major change in organizations is well established and goes like this:

The Change Sequence

An analysis of the major organizational changes of recent years reveals an almost invariable sequence of events:

Fright: The organization is faced with unmistakable signs of alarm: Imminent bankruptcy, a slump in sales, major strikes, a squeeze in margins, and massive operational difficulties might be some of them.

New People: New people are brought in to the top of the organization, most frequently a new chief executive, to do the necessary and often painful restructuring. Because there is a need for incisive action, quick decisions with inadequate information, and a certain ruthlessness, the new person at the top is often a Zeus character.

New Directions: The new team at the top reorganizes priorities. Some lines of activity, or some products, are dropped, and others are started. Bits of the organization may be sold off or closed down, so that everything can be concentrated on the best of what is left. A new strategy emerges.

New Groupings: The new strategy leads to new structures, which in turn mean individuals changing roles and responsibilities. New methods and systems are simultaneously introduced.

Only in the case of *additive change,* in which an organization of its own accord takes on another component, does it seem possible to avoid this traumatic sequence. It seems that it needs an organizational earthquake to change the balance of gods when things are going wrong. (An excellent analysis of the causes and process of forced organizational change is provided by Stuart Slatter in *Corporate Recovery* [London: Penguin, 1984].)

Linking the Gods

Given the right mix, the organization still needs to be held together. The gods need to be linked. Failed linkages in institutions show up most dramatically in the scrapbook of "goofs" held in the institutional memory of any organization—the creations of the research department developed by someone else, the sales drive that ran out of goods to sell, the product switch that no one mentioned to the purchasing department, and so on. More insistently, they show up in the arguments, bickerings, and tribal wars that proliferate in organizations, particularly the bigger ones.

Cultural harmony in one part of the organization is often nurtured and supported by deliberately distinguishing it from the other parts. Enmity without encourages harmony within. But this cultural isolation can destroy the total institution. Linkage among the cultures is essential, and effective linkage has three elements: cultural tolerance, bridges, and a common language. When these fail, a fourth element, slack, covers up the cracks, but slack is only the thermometer of inefficiency or incompetence, the outcome of mixed-up management.

Cultural Tolerance

Each culture has its own preferred ways of coordinating and controlling. The club cultures rely on trust, empathy, and personal inspection. The role culture links defined jobs or roles by means of rules and procedures and an inspection system to make sure that the rules and procedures are enforced. Task cultures, dealing always with new problems, plan and replan, using past data to correct future estimates and forecasts. Existential cultures relegate and delegate the coordinating function, calling it *administration* (a denigrating term for them).

But as I have shown, since the ways of one culture are anathema to another, the personal visitation of a Zeus seems to an Apollonian to be an intrusion on private territory, reeking of distrust: "Doesn't he believe my reports or understand the figure?" Zeus people, on the other hand, are bored by the formalities of Apollonian coordinating mechanisms and find them hard to use. The discussions and committees that lie behind the planning of Athenians seem like inefficiency to Apollonians, just as the disregard of Dionysians seems like irresponsibility.

But to impose your ways on others is bigotry, cultural sin. The first step, then, to effective linkage is to allow each part of the organization to develop its own appropriate methods of coordination and control and to tolerate differences among the cultures. Otherwise, one enters the "spiral of distrust," when what seems sensible coordination to one person appears intrusive control to the other.

The Spiral of Distrust

The principle of "balance" keeps cropping up in life. There seems to be a reciprocal "balancing" relationship between trust and control, so that where trust is increased, control diminishes, and if control is increased the perceived trust is decreased, as on the balance illustrated below.

The farmer had been successful; he now operated three smallholdings (each about 120 acres) in addition to his own home farm. Each smallholding was managed by one of his three sons (indeed, he had bought the farms for this purpose). Clearly, he thought, good management required that he coordinate the work of the four farms so that he would get optimal use of the central pool of capital equipment, better purchasing and sales deals, and so on. The principle was so obvious that he didn't need to discuss it; he merely asked his sons for a weekly detailed advanced schedule of their work, followed up a week later by a matching report on work done with, where appropriate, details of quantities.

The sons met in the house of the eldest. "Father has been conning us along," one said. "He told us that he trusted us to run our own farms and would finance the start-up. Now it's clear that he wants to check on everything we do both before and after we do it. We are just employees—not his trusted sons. I propose that we demand that he hand over to us the legal ownership of our

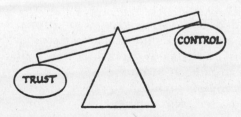

farms, or otherwise he is likely to sell them over our heads once we've put them in order." "And another thing," said the third son, "he's deliberately adding together all the proceeds so that we can't tell whose is what."

The father was astonished. His attempts to start his sons off as independent farmers had resulted in outright rebellion. It must, he muttered, be the result of this new mood of distrust and independence in the youth of the country.

The possibility that his well-meant attempts at coordination looked like control, which suggested, in that Zeus-like culture, a measure of distrust, simply did not occur to him.

The spiral of distrust starts with good intentions and is often invisible.

But cultural tolerance is only the prerequisite, the necessary condition, of a balanced organization. Much more, of a more positive nature, is needed to link the cultures.

Bridges

Some well-known work in organization theory has demonstrated that the more "differentiation" there is among the people, the work, the ideologies, and the time horizons of different parts of an organization, the more methods of "integration" will be needed.[4] The idea of balance again. Like many of the precepts of organization theory, this is blindingly obvious once it has been stated. In our terms, the more diverse the cultures are, the more bridges will be needed.

Bridges range from copies of correspondence, through joint committees (with appeals to superior courts or umpires), to coordinating individuals, liaison groups, or project teams. In between them are what might be called *pontoons,* or the temporary bridges of task forces, study groups, or "confrontation meetings" between the arguing groups.

Without bridges, the cultures go their separate ways (resulting usually in lowered efficiency and the occasional goof), or they must be held together at the top by imposed directives, decrees, and refereelike decisions. Using the top of the organization as the principal "bridge" not only distorts the structure and corrupts the cultures but also occupies an undue proportion of the top people's time.

The Paradox of Delegation

The chief executive was explaining his method of management.

"I've taken my job," he said, "which is running the organization, I suppose, and then I've split it into its constituent parts (such as planning, financial control, and sales) and then put a man in charge of each. That way I've delegated my total work and am free to act as a counselor, consultant, or arbitrator to any of them as and when needed. Look," he added, "an empty desk, an empty diary: perfect delegation, wouldn't you say?"

Three months later I saw him again.

"How's it working?" I asked.

"The system's fine," he replied, "it's the people, they're not up to it. They have a very narrow focus, can't take an overall perspective. Do you think they can be educated to think like directors of the company?"

"How do you mean?" I asked.

"Well, everything I suggest to them seems to come back to me as an argument to be resolved. Our board meetings consist of a set of functional viewpoints, leaving me to take the company view and make the decision. They can't see beyond their own function, yet in their position every functional problem concerns others as well as themselves."

But that's what you wanted, wasn't it?" I asked. "You delegated everything except coordination, compromise, and linkage, so that remains your job."

"I suppose that's true," he said ruefully. "But it wasn't what I intended. Now I'm busier than I ever was before I delegated it all so neatly. I'm so busy I don't have time to think, let alone be counselor, consultant, and all those other things I talked about. I've gotten back more than I gave away; it's like delegating into the wind."

"Perhaps you should try delegating some of your linkage responsibility as well as your functional supervision. After all, if you can cross the river only at its top, not only will it be a very busy bridge, but other people also will have to do a lot of walking."

The *matrix organization* (in which the demands for cooperation among functions are met by full-time project groups made up of representatives from the functions, operating under the project leaders) is the ultimate "bridged" organization. In this design, the functions' cultural priorities are exported to the project groups. In these groups, much depends on the leadership capacity of the project leader to make an effective bridge, bonding the capabilities of the functions to a common good. He is helped in this task if he has the power of selection and/or promotion; if the projects control the allocation of new investment; and if the project group has the full use of each individual's time. On the other hand, putting too much emphasis on the "bridge" may weaken the individual cultures or functions. The balance can be restored by giving back some of the powers (of appointment or production) to the functions or by retaining them for the center or top of the organization. This will weaken the power of the projects but strengthen the functions. It has been argued that in a matrix organization, projects pursue the practical and functions pursue the ideal. Balance would suggest the need for a constantly shifting distribution between these two.

Few organizations find that the complexity justifies the cost of a full matrix organization. Few are content with a bridge only at the top. Most locate a bridge at the points of major interaction between the cultures—where research meets production, for instance, or where purchasing, production, and sales combine in a production schedule. Some include bridges between policy management and executive supervision. The first question clearly is, how many bridges and where? The temptation for management is always to overdo it. It feels lonely at the top when you don't know what is going on or know who does know. The danger of too much coordination is not only its cost but also the ever-lurking spiral of distrust. The danger of too little is, of course, the goofs and suboptimization referred to earlier. On balance, experience would suggest that we make do with as little as we can, even at the risk of a goof. There is an established connection between the quantity of coordination and the degree of apathy in organizations. The more coordination there is, the greater the apathy will be. The invisible apathy may well cost more than the occasional but visible goof. If of course, goofs are either illegal (e.g., in hospitals or government) or extremely costly, the apathy may have to be endured.

The second decision to be made about bridging is the method. There are essentially three ways of achieving formal coordination in organizations, by *grouping, central information,* or *liaison.*

Grouping

Grouping essentially means putting all the functions concerned with a problem into one group with one objective. In a factory, instead of having a production unit serviced by engineers, quality control, maintenance, and production development, there is one of each of these in the unit, so that all the bits to be coordinated are represented there. The matrix organization applies this method in the extreme. It is effective but clearly very expensive, since to work it properly you need to have an engineer, quality controller, maintenance officer, and development officer for each group or problem.

Central Information

By means of central information, all the information necessary for coordination is routed, by manual documentation or computer, to a central point, usually at that position in the hierarchy that could be called the lowest crossover point in the organization chart of the points to be linked. In a predictable world, it is possible to work out what information is needed when and where, in order to allow particular decisions to be made. One can even state in advance the criteria for these decisions, so that they can be made automatically by the computer when the decision is at hand. The impact of the computer on organizational decision making (as opposed to record keeping) is here, in this form of bridging. The airline booking operations, the computerized stock-control systems, and even the automatic entry gates to parking lots rely on this vertical information system of linkage. Central information works well in predictable situations if the humans involved can live up to the accuracy required. Most systems, however, are overdesigned and vulnerable to human error. One fool can gum up the whole works.

Liaison

Liaison is the most tenuous form of bridge. It relies on one man telling another what he is doing, wants to do, or cannot do. Liaison can be helped along by the disciplines of committees, by formally circulated information, or by permanent liaison officers (a sort of human bridge), but ultimately it depends on the willingness of individuals to talk, discuss, and compromise on both means and ends.

There are cultural affinities to these bridges. The Athenian culture prefers liaison, with its flexibility and emphasis on trust and informal ways. Apollo cultures like central information and the certainty and predictability that this involves. And Zeus cultures, quite properly, like the group, with all that they need under their own command.

But organizations remain a cultural mix and require a variety of bridging mechanisms. The temptation is to overdo one's preferred mechanism and to attempt to apply it to the other cultures. The tidiness of the data and the forms of central information cannot apply throughout the organization without reducing its flexibility. Apollonians must show some cultural tolerance in their bridges with the task cultures. Zeus cultures must allow more systematization than they are comfortable with. One must, in short, resist the instinctual pull of one's one culture if the bridge is with another culture.

The cultural split implied by bridging two different cultures occurs in its most obvious form in the role of the liaison man who must stand with a foot in each. The *integrator*, as he has been called, has become a prized person in the complex organizations of today—and a special person. The successful liaison man, we know from research, is familiar with each of the areas he has to bridge and is respected by both, has a high status in the organization so that he can get things done, is skilled in interpersonal relationships, and has a high tolerance for stress. Not a job for a weakling! Nor for a very young man or for someone who has failed in the mainstream. The stress arises, in my view, from the great difficulty of having to live in two cultures simultaneously. It is hard to sustain this dual nationality. Most liaison men become identified in time with one side or the other, thus reducing their efficiency as a bridge and turning liaison into negotiation. A better understanding of the cultures and their preferences might make it easier for these human bridges to carry out their very difficult but necessary role.

Nowadays the supervisor and the junior manager are often liaison men parading under more formal titles. Their job is to link a number of lateral forces, often without the formal authority to do so. It is at their level that the asterisk situations that I referred to earlier arise—situations in which the possible is to be preferred to the ideal, trust and intuition and empathy are quicker than formal communication, and interpersonal relationships are critical: Zeus situations, in fact. Good liaison men are Zeus characters, but they often act as bridges between Athenian task forces. They need cultural self-discipline.

Any inhabitant of organizations will have perceived the law of the pendulum at work as the organization centralizes, then a few years later decentralizes, only to centralize again in due course. Here the organization is intuitively searching for a new balance: It swings from central information to a mixture of groups and liaison and back again. The search for balance never ends. The swinging is inevitable, but if done with cultural understanding, the pain is less.

A Common Language

The third aspect of linkage is a common language. "An organization that talks together walks together," one might say. But the vocabulary of organizations differs from our everyday conversation. What is it that goes across the various bridges in the linking systems? What does the organization choose to talk about? Is it sales? Or costs? Or productivity? What concealed but central values are revealed by its private codes or the fashionable jargon of the day?

What are the critical figures or columns in the formal reporting system? Do the internal memoranda refer to people, reports, or departments? What does the private humor reveal as the "in" buzzwords? What are the failures you must not make?

A supervisor was studying the forty pages of internal information circulated monthly to all departments of the great integrated multidepartment corporation. "Do you use all this?" he was asked. "Oh, no," he replied. "I only look at this figure on page 22. If it's up I'm OK, down and I'm in trouble."

The choice of what you count, what you compare with what, what you show to whom, has a clear effect on your behavior. Do you compare performance with past performance or with planned performance? Do you count functional results or overall results? There is little point in talking profits if the reporting system counts only sales and costs except at the very top.

The code indicates where the power lies and what method of linkage is most important.

Organizational Codes

An internal memo in a Zeus culture often reads like a private family letter. For example, "In view of Jerry's information, JGH suggested that we suggest to Bob H. that he try to win over Peter McK. in the hope that his support will be conclusive. RTC agreed to follow this up after talking to TStJR and GJS."

Apollonian communiques bristle with terms like MKR/Z, PROD/EVR/S, JDRs, and FSPs, which refer to departments or regular documentary returns.

Task cultures are full of commando language: Bill's gang, the television group, the forward planning people.

Dionysians use professional rather than organization codes, demonstrating their true allegiance.

All these codes are baffling to the outsider, but they do serve a function in linking the organization together, as long as both sides understand them. Language, however, can be a barrier as much as a bridge.

The slang, buzzwords, and jargon point to current priorities: "objectives," "participation," "quality," or "health and cleanliness."

It is easy to be quietly humorous about the languages of organizations, but words do affect behavior. Language is normally but a mirror of its society, but it can be used more deliberately to shape and direct the preoccupations and priorities of that society or to reinforce new bridging mechanisms. For instance, if a "group" system is introduced, the reporting mechanism must reflect the new system by producing "group" data. If quality is more important than quantity, the informal vocabulary should reflect that. And the languages should coincide. It is no use preaching productivity to the unions if the statistical vocabulary does not contain appropriate productivity statistics. You can detect an organization's heart by looking at its language.

The temptation is to follow one's personal cultural instincts. The quandary is how far to "sin," to go against the instincts in the interests of cultural propriety, to use new vocabularies delib erately to send new messages, in order to achieve a new internal balance in the organization. The instinct of a Zeus to rely on informal conversations to inject new values and goals may not carry over to the Apollonian part of the organization, which will expect these changes to be reflected in the statistics of the reporting system. Athenians won't believe them unless they are incorporated in revised group assignments.

Slack, the Price of Imbalance

If linkage is not achieved, the gaps will be filled in by slack, and organizational slack indicates some fat somewhere in the system. A small degree of slack is not a bad thing; for a completely lean organization finds it hard to cope with any irregularities in its planned activities. Slack can be used to iron out bumps, to live through difficult periods, and to take advantage of unexpected opportunities. But slack that conceals poor linkage or a mismatch of gods is a cancer in the body of the organized society. Like cancer, it can grow unnoticed, until it becomes so bad that the whole body begins to decay. By then, it is too often too late to intervene.

Slack takes various forms:

Investment: Equipment and facilities are provided to cope with the peaks of quality or quantity, leaving "slack" in the troughs.

Seasonal industries (e.g., soft drinks, photofinishing, tourism) invest for summer peaks. Quality-conscious industries tool up for the highest quality, even if such small tolerances are required only for a small portion of their work.

Staffing: Many organizations staff up to meet all contingencies, including sickness and holidays as well as peak loading. Industries that peak daily (catering, commuter transport) have a daily slack problem. Slack in staff can create self-fulfilling prophecies: Overrecruitment to cover wastage can actually encourage it, as people see a visible excess and leave before they are pushed.

Systems: Systems can be designed to cope with an expanded operation but may not adapt to the varying size of the operation, and so a small workload incurs the full weight of coordination, systems, and controls, or trivial decisions receive the full board-room policy routine.

Time: The more time you have at your disposal, the less you need of other forms of slack. In the quality furniture trade, it is customary to manufacture only when a customer's order is firm. This practice allows one to carry minimum stocks (no investment slack) but makes production planning very difficult, so that one probably must carry excess personnel (staffing slack).

Margins: High margins permit one to carry other types of slack, including error slack. Technologies to which speed is more important than accuracy (e.g., trading) often carry high margins to allow for error slack. It is an established fact that stock-market ratings of earnings per share rise in relation to the likelihood of risk or error. It is then the customer who pays.

Errors: Error slack usually accompanies high margins, on the assumption that the errors will be corrected. The existence of room for errors in the tradition of the industry allows one to skimp on systems but, of course, results in poor quality and shoddy work if the errors are not corrected in time.

We can choose our slack, although usually we fall into line with the traditions of our industry, occupation, or society. It can be argued that Britain's tradition of using staffing slack rather than investment slack has been a major contributor to its successive economic crises. Labor has historically been cheap in Britain, and investment was more lucratively routed overseas to the old empire. As a result, British firms tended to be overmanned and underequipped, compared with, for example, the United States, where capital was readily available and labor scarce. Now, of course, the labor slack in Britain is no longer cheap. In cutting down that slack, a pool of unemployment has been created, but, and possibly more serious, the slack has not been replaced by investment slack. Margin slack is seldom possible in the conditions of international competition (although continual devaluations can help), thus leaving any needs for slack to be met by time (overdue delivery dates), error (poor quality), or high domestic prices. The organized society pays for its slack through its consumers.

On an organizational scale, there are cultural preferences for slack. Club cultures prefer margin slack. This offers room for experiment, allows people to learn by their mistakes without ruining the institution, and permits flexibility. When appropriate they would like to back this up with investment slack as a form of equipment backup to their key resource—people.

Role cultures believe in system and staffing slack. In their way of thinking, the capital assets of the operation can be used efficiently or inefficiently depending on the way the work is planned and carried out. They like to play on the slack of human resources (believing these to be the most flexible of resources) and on chains of systems. The ability to draw at will on a pool of retained labor has, for instance, long been at the heart of the automobile industry's way of working.

Task cultures like investment slack—again as equipment for their talents to work on—and time. If time is not available, they tend to staff up: More brainpower produces good results more quickly.

Luckily, existential cultures have small linkage requirements. Luckily, because these cultures seldom have the resources to create investment slack, they abhor systems slack and are unlikely to add deliberately to their number to create staffing slack. When therefore, the Dionysians of an existential culture must be coordinated, usually delays (time slack) or mistakes (error slack) are the result.

When the comparative costs of the different forms of slack change, as they did in Britain in the 1990s, management must reconsider, and often act against, its cultural instincts. Club cultures, for instance, are often accustomed to working in a mini-monopoly situation in which for reasons of geography (they are in a regionally distant market), size (they are too small to bother with), or custom (the norms of the cartel, industry, or occupation), they have price discretion and could use the slack of high margins. When they expand, they encounter competition and have to cut slack in order to compete. If they do not at the same time improve their linkage, they will have to find another form of slack. If they are not careful, that slack will be of the time or error variety. Thus growth in Zeus cultures can often result in inefficiency.

Role cultures, used to a pool of cheap labor and with decision routines that examine investment projects with a microscope while overlooking major staffing decisions, may have to change their ways if the pool becomes expensive and can no longer be fished at will. Investment may then be the appropriate form of slack if linkage fails.

Labor as a Fixed Cost

A friend was attending an international management course in Belgium. The British executives were complaining loudly and long that management in Britain had become impossible owing to the burden of legislation and the impossibility of moving one's labor force around or reducing it as one wanted.

"Aw, shucks!" said an American. "We've lived with that situation in Scandinavia for years. It's easy. You just treat your labor as a fixed cost."

There was a perplexed silence.

"And so . . . ?" asked a timid voice.

"Why, then your investment is your variable. You build lots of small plants and close down or open whole plants. Play around with the operation, not the people."

It's only a change in slack.

The Role of the Missionary Manager

Cultural propriety might appear to be a rather obvious virtue. Surely every organization intuitively reacts to the influencing forces in its environment and seeks to minimize inappropriate forms of slack? Indeed, if it does not, won't it be starved of profit and therefore of its prospects for survival? Why, then shouldn't a purely mercenary approach be the best way of securing that cultural propriety, which will in turn remove any unwanted slack or unnecessary incompetence?

This is the essential premise of capitalism. I shall argue at more length later that this premise will not hold much longer. Here we can at least recognize that the principle is fallible even now. It is true that gross incompetence or excessive slack usually results in a loss of clients and thence in organizational death, given a free market. But how many markets are free? For a start, all professions have a protected market, as do all government agencies. These are organizations just like any others and often affect people's lives more deeply than do those of commerce and industry. Incompetence or slack in these areas is protected by regulation—a slow-moving and ineffective device, particularly when, as in the case of the professions, the police, and the civil service, it is self-policed. Then the industrial and commercial organizations owned by the state normally have protected markets, at least in their own countries. There are exceptions, notably the automobile industries in France, Britain, and Germany, but the exceptions are rare enough to be noticeable. Finally, in the private sector of commerce and industry, how effective a policeman is competition among rivals? Where monopoly is outlawed, most businesspeople would prefer an oligopoly in which a number of firms run *parallel* businesses, competing in defined ways in defined areas but usually mirroring one another's cultural patterns. True competition comes from outside, from another country or another technology carrying with it different assumptions about cultures and slack. And when that true competition arrives, there is no shortage of squeals of anguish and pleas for tarriff barriers and technological protection (once it was for textile workers, now for shoemakers).

Profit—the major mercenary objective—is more easily guaranteed by seeking to win an area of price discretion than by eliminating slack. In these days, when profit margins are increasingly regulated, decreased costs can actually result in decreased profits. Indeed, profit can be the result of inefficiency rather than efficiency, in a situation in which *margins,* but not the final price, are controlled.

Profit as the Measure of Inefficiency

In my early days in the oil industry, a marketing cartel still operated in various parts of the world, a cartel in which the major companies agreed to preserve their existing market shares in each territory (the "As Is" agreement).

Under this arrangement, the oil companies became essentially monopoly distribution systems for a vital commodity: justifiable, perhaps, in an age when oil supplies were limited and capital could have been wasted in unnecessary fields at the consumer end. However, profit was still used as the measure of efficiency.

One of my first tasks was to compile the price lists for lubricating oils. It was a simple task, actually. There was a printed list of cost items for each brand. I got the relevant figures from the Accounts Department and added on the 15 percent profit margin (not excessive; the companies saw themselves as nonexploitative), and put the final total down as the new price.

After a couple of weeks, I commented to the sales manager that this system was a recipe for inefficiency, since the higher our costs were the higher would be the 15 percent margin. He was horrified at the thought. Conditioned to believe that higher profit was always good, he could not bring himself to consider that it might indicate only inefficiency in a monopolistic service industry.

This particular cartel ended soon afterward when oil supplies increased and the companies began searching for new markets. The counterparts to this story continue, however, in many industries and trades in many pockets of society.

In most Western countries, over 50 percent of their gross domestic product is already in the public sector with protected markets. If an honest evaluation were made of the remainder, a large part would consist of professional fees, practical oligopolies of parallel businesses, or territorial monopolies equivalent to the small regional equipment rental operation or the village store whose monopoly is too small for others to wish to intervene. All these areas have price discretion to some degree. The discipline of competition and the whip of profit punishes only gross incompetence or excessive slack. Cultural propriety, like social propriety cannot be enforced, only desired. Mercenary organizations and mercenary managers are not in themselves enough. They must be missionaries, too, if incompetence—mixed-up management, that first dilemma of the organized society—is to be resolved.

4

The Gods
in Their Settings

People are different, as we have noted, and different personalities favor different gods. But it goes further and deeper than that. An organization is not only a culture in itself; it also is surrounded by a culture, be it of Japan or Italy, of schoolteaching or medicine. The *setting* in which an organization operates has a major impact on the blend of gods, even if the demands of size, life cycles, and work patterns all seem to push it in another direction. Management works best when it goes with the grain of its surrounding culture, not with the dictates of logic. We should, therefore, expect to see a different balance of gods in different countries and in different occupations, and we should not necessarily expect to be able to replicate Japanese ways in America or the practices of business in a church.

We do, as it happens, know something about national differences in management style; we have some clues to the nature of successful Japanese organizations and successful American businesses; and we are beginning to understand the essential differences between, for instance, schools and volunteer groups as organizations. In this chapter, we say a little about each to emphasize that the theory of cultural propriety must take account of the setting of the organization as well as the work to be done. It also is important to understand that the gods and the cultures they

Dionysus Turned Zeus?

represent apply in their different ways to all organizations, not just to those of business or of the United States.

National Differences

Geert Hofstede spent six years trying to pin down the essential differences among national cultures.[1] He looked at and compared all the other studies (thirteen of them) that had tried to do the same thing, but he also hit on a neat idea: He persuaded IBM to let him interview some of their personnel in forty different countries. Since they all worked for the same corporation in similar jobs, any differences in their cultural attitudes would most likely be due to their national differences, not to their occupation. Hofstede is, of course, dealing with norms and generalizations—not all Mexicans are alike, but they may, most of them, have certain characteristics in common.

He came up with four distinguishing features:

Power: Some nationalities like and approve of hierarchies, whereas others want everyone to be as equal as possible. Some want everyone to be independent, but others accept that most should be dependent on others. Hofstede measured people on their preference for power distance.

Uncertainty: Some societies are more worried by uncertainty and risk than others are. They like rules, stable careers, and fixed patterns of life. They accept that there are experts, and they listen to them. Hofstede classified cultures on an uncertainty avoidance scale.

Individualism: Some societies favor a loose social framework, in which individuals are supposed to look after themselves. Other societies want more collectivism, tighter, closer families, and organizations that look after them and in return expect their loyalty. Hofstede's scale ran from individualism at one end to collectivism at the other.

Masculinity: Some countries are more "masculine" in their attitudes, valuing assertiveness and the acquisition of money and things and not caring for the quality of life or other people. Other nationalities were the opposite, veering toward more "feminine" values. Interestingly, the more "masculine" a society is as a whole, the wider the gap will be between the way the men and women in it think.

When Hofstede groups nationalities together, it is clear that he is on to something. It is also clear that there are implications for the mix of gods. For instance:

Southeast Asia is happy with hierarchy and power and is able to live with uncertainty. By these measures, Singapore, Hong Kong, India, and the Philippines are lands fit for Zeus, and the entrepreneurial organizations of this region seem to bear that out.

Americans, British, and Scandinavians do not mind uncertainty, but they are far more democratic than Southeast Asia is, suggesting more of a penchant for Athena, a suggestion supported by the scores compiled by British executives in answering the questionnaire at the end of Chapter 2. Athena is the personal choice of most of them, even though few find that their organizations' scores bear this out.

The Americans are also, however, strongly individualist (Dionysian), a fact that will become important in the future, as the next chapter emphasizes, whereas the Scandinavians are more collectivist, which can be a polite word for conformist.

The Japanese are very different. They dislike uncertainty and are very collectivist, as opposed to individualist, masculine rather than feminine, and rather neutral about power. It is a culture made for families and Apollo—exactly what we find in practice. They are likely to be efficient but not entrepreneurial, to be conformist and materialistic, not eccentric.

France likes power and hierarchy, is individualist but not risk taking; Zeus sitting on top of Apollo, and in the middle. Management is full of rules interrupted by crises.

Countries like Austria and Germany, which dislike uncertainty, want equality but not individualism and espouse masculine and material values, are asking for Apollonian institutions tempered by formal democratic procedures, which is what they have. They are hardworking, efficient, and egalitarian but also conformist and, with notable exceptions, unadventurous and even unexciting.

Managing by Objectives, Cross-culturally

Management by objectives (MBO) has been a favorite American and British tool of management. It does, however, as Hofstede points out, depend on certain assumptions that may not work outside the United States and Britain.[2]

MBO assumes that subordinate and superior can negotiate (not power conscious). It also assumes that results are important (masculinity) and that some risks are worth taking (uncertainty) which are the individual's responsibility (individualism). MBO is made for Athenians.

In France, its equivalent, DPPO (Direction participation par objectife), never caught on. The French are accustomed to arbitrary and personal leadership, which creates dependent behavior and an unwillingness to take individual risks. Apollo studded with Zeus is no place for negotiated contracts.

In Germany, MBO has been formalized and transformed into management by joint goal setting—a democratized Apollonian revision of the original.

These cultural stereotypes can, of course, be taken too far. Not every German or American fits the pattern. There are many entrepreneurial German firms, whereas Japan, as we shall see, is dependent not only on its large organizations but also on a host of small independent businesses. The other factors—size, life cycles, and work patterns—also emphasize the choice of gods and their mix. Nevertheless, the surrounding culture is important. As we shall see in the next chapter, the crisis facing organizations in Britain and the United States is caused by the conflict among the kinds of organizations that reason and logic would give us and those that the cultures of democracy and individualism are prepared to live with.

Trust is Better Than Contracts

The overseas Chinese businessman—typically a Zeus at heart—prefers to deal without written contracts. If you need a contract, he argues, to keep a man to his obligations, then you should not be doing business with him in the first place.

It follows that overseas Chinese businessmen cannot afford to try to squeeze out all they can get from customers or contractors, because there is no enforceable contract to fall back on. Instead, they must try to negotiate deals in which both parties benefit, so that it is in nobody's interest to default or delay.

That sort of trust comes slowly. The overseas Chinese starts with small orders and small contracts when he does not know you. If you demonstrate trust, the orders will grow.

The idea, however, that success means a deal in which each side wins is not always understood in Western cultures.

The Gods in Japan

The best test of cultural differences between nations is to try to apply Japanese management practices to American organizations. If the surrounding setting does matter, then what works in Japan may well not work in America, and vice versa. The principles of management may not be as universal as some would like. The differences between Japanese and American organizations are great, which does not mean, of course, that they cannot learn something from each other. "Quality circles," after all, were invented in America before being taken up and developed to their full potential in Japan and then reexported to America.

A Japanese organization is built on a fundamental contract of trust between an individual and an organization. The individual trusts the organization to employ him (very seldom her) for life, to reward him better as he grows older and more senior, and to use him and his talents appropriately. In return, he puts the immediate requirements of the organization before his own, being prepared to change jobs, locations, and even careers if the organization requires it. It has to be a contract of trust, because formal contracts for longer than one year are actually forbidden by law.

Because of this blend of security and flexibility, the organization can operate a proper Apollonian culture, a culture in which the individual fits into the role and the system that logic would require. In Western eyes, this can make the Japanese sound like human robots, replaceable human parts, but it does not feel like that if the organization is viewed as a caring family for which, because your long-term interests are guaranteed, it is no sacrifice but, rather, a privilege and a pleasure to do your duty in that role to which it has pleased the organization to call you. In its present form, the Apollonian contract is not one in which the organization *uses* the individual but one in which there is a long-term identity of interest between the organization and all the people in it.

The Japanese Assembly Room

William Ouchi describes the experience of an American electronics firm that opened a manufacturing plant in Japan.[3] In the final assembly area of the plant, young Japanese women wired together electronic products on a piece-rate system: The more they wired, the more they were paid. About two months after opening, the supervisors approached the plant manager. "Honorable plant manager," they said humbly as they bowed, "we are embarrassed to be so forward, but we must speak to you, because all the girls have threatened to quit work this Friday." "Why," they wanted to know, "can't our plant have the same compensation system as other Japanese companies? When you hire a new girl, her starting salary should be fixed by her age. An eighteen-year-old should be paid more than a sixteen-year-old. Every year on her birthday she should receive an automatic increase in her pay. The idea that any one of us can be more productive than another must be wrong, because none of us in final assembly could make anything unless all the other people in the plant had done their jobs right first. To single out one person as being more productive is wrong and is also personally humiliating to us."

The company changed its compensation system.

The Japanese, it is true, run a very sophisticated version of Apollo in order to keep it familylike and human. Roles, for instance, are deliberately kept ambiguous and overlapping. There are few of the detailed job descriptions in which Western Apollonian organizations abound; instead, the responsibility for any task is spread across a number of roles, and it is understood that the responsibility for all the tasks is shared by all the roles in a group. This works only if the individual bits of the organization are kept small enough, but the sense of collective responsibility that results is a guarantee against the negative power typical of Apollo cultures. But the groups that result in Japanese organizations are subtly different from the Athenian groups of Western institutions. These are not the problem-solving task forces of skilled individuals but collections of roles doing prescribed tasks. The "role family" that is produced is the basic building block of Japanese organizations, and much care, time, and trouble goes into the nurture and maintenance of these organization families. Asked about his job, a Japanese will name his group rather than his particular job and will spend maybe two hours a week after hours socializing with his work group. Apollonian temples built of role families are very human places *if* you are happy to give over part of your identity to such a family and such a temple. Japanese organizations are "total" organizations, and "total" organizations, as William Ouchi points out, are equated in the West with prisons, hospitals, military establishments, and such. They are not, in other words, the preferred cultures of the West. Apollonian temples of the excellence seen in Japan can be built only in a land where security is more important than individualism and where organizational success counts for more than personal advancement— the kind of values that Hofstede found in his research on Japan.

Japanese organizations do, however, go to great lengths to reinforce their side of the Apollonian contract. They consciously build up the image and the tradition of the corporation, admittedly using Apollonian devices like the company song, company training schools, and company slogans. They reinforce the image not only with the promise of a secure career but also with a compensation system that pays approximately half of each person's total remuneration as a six-monthly bonus tied to the results of the total organization and each person's basic salary. It is the corporation's success, not one's own, that counts, and this is outwardly symbolized by the fact that everyone wears the same uniform and that no one has a reserved parking place or a special place to eat. The individual should see himself as part of a group and as a proud member of a great corporation, one that serves him as well as being served by him.

The organization also serves the individual by providing him with a career. It is not usually a specialist career but one that moves the individual from role to role and place to place. This breeds more versatile, flexible, and rounded people and also, of course, people who will find it less easy to leave the corporation, which matters not at all *if* you trust the organization with your career. The career system is, therefore, a powerful bonding device. So is the decisionmaking system.

Decisions in Japanese organizations are not made by the top man or by a special group. Instead, quite logically, all the roles involved have their say, though not, however, in a committee, in which many have to be silent so that one can speak, but through the *nemawashi* and *ringi* systems. *Nemawashi* requires the informal contribution of everyone interested and involved at the discussion phase. *Ringi* requires that every decision first be circulated to all relevant roles for their approval or comment and be recirculated if in the process an alternative comes up. It is time-consuming, but by bonding every role into the decision, it is another way of preempting any possible use of blocking or negative power. In the end, although the Japanese take an age to decide anything, once decided, it can be implemented immediately.

The Japanese may be devout and very sensible followers of Apollo, but they do not ignore the other gods. Richard Pascale and Anthony Athos, in their book on Japanese management,[4] provide a detailed description of Matsushita (producer of National, Panasonic, and Technics brands) and make it quite clear that the founder, Konosuke Matsushita, was a Zeus when he started the business in his living room in 1918 and remained a Zeus more than sixty years later when although nominally retired, he intervened to appoint a new chief executive because he deemed it to be necessary. Matsushita, perhaps because of its Zeus-like history, has an original way of allocating overheads to the ancillary divisions. It doesn't. Instead, it requires each division to pay a tax of 60 percent of its gross profits to the center but allows it to keep the remaining 40 percent to reinvest in its own future. The 60 percent tax is expected to cover overheads and also to finance the center's venture capital fund. It is a system that provides room for Zeus figures in a tight Apollonian framework. Japan also has its product development groups and its planners and researchers, who fit into the Athenian problem-solving mode, as do its renowned and much-imitated quality circles—Athena on the shop floor.

A Japanese Speaking

"One thing you notice rather quickly is that everyone who comes here [Toyota] with any experience soon leaves. . . . Sometimes I wonder if those who quit are normal and human, while we who remain are the abnormal ones. Those who stay seem to lack self-respect. If you want to think and act independently, you can't stay."
Dionysians do not fit.

If you want a lesson in how to run an Apollonian system without encountering the perils of impersonality, blocking tactics, inertia, and lack of creativity, go to Japan. But the extremes to which the Japanese go would not be possible unless the surrounding culture were also Apollonian, one in which the individual was content, even proud, to be but a small part of a large whole and was prepared to make present sacrifices for future security. NSK, which set up a plant in the northeast of Britain to manufacture ball bearings for Europe under Japanese management but with a British workforce, overlaid the strong Apollonian culture with an Athenian task culture, which set store by the professional engineers and encouraged problem-solving groups at all levels. This may have been a response to the requirements of an evolving technology and a difficult market, but it would undoubtedly help to make the dominant Apollonian ethos more tolerable to the more individualist Britishers.

Educating for Apollo

Life can be tough for a child in Japan. To get into one of the great organizations, it is almost essential to graduate from one of the good national or private universities. The courses at all high schools are identical in content, so the pressure on formal examinations is enormous—there is no other criterion available for success.

Parents therefore go to great lengths to get their children into the best nursery school, so that they may from there get into a good primary school, because only then will they have a chance of entering one of the top high schools and universities. At four years of age, reports William Ouchi, many children of ambitious parents go to special summer schools, eight hours a day, to get special coaching just to take the entrance exam for that one nursery school.[6]

Education, too, is Apollonian, leaving little room for individual differences or deviations from the system.

The Gods in America

American organizations are different. In America, the Apollonian organization has been made viable not by turning its parts into role families but by infiltrating it whenever possible with Athenians and aspirers after Zeus. It is true that some corporations, notably perhaps IBM, have sought to emulate the Japanese and to become "total organizations" in their own way, and many have been successful, but it has not been the usual American way.

Listen to some of Peters and Waterman's recipes for excellence, arrived at after studying America's most successful companies:[7]

A Bias for Action: "When we've got a big problem here, we grab ten senior guys and stick them in a room for a week. They come up with an answer and implement it" (p.13).
(Athenians?)

"The action-oriented bits and pieces come under many labels—champions, teams, task forces, czars, projects centers, skunk works and quality circles" (p. 126).
(Zeus and Athena?)

Autonomy and Entrepreneurship: "3M . . . seems not a large corporation but rather a loose network of laboratories and cubbyholes populated by feverish inventors and dauntless entrepreneurs" (p. 14).
(Zeus and Dionysians?)

"They don't try to hold everyone on so short a rein that he can't be creative. They encourage practical risk-taking and support good tries" (p. 14).
(Zeus?)

Productivity Through People: "The excellent companies have a deeply ingrained philosophy that says, in effect, "Respect the individual," "Make people winners," "Let them stand out," "Treat people as adults" (p. 15).
(Everyone a Dionysian or a Zeus?)

Simple Form, Lean Staff: "The . . . structural form should be based on "three pillars," each one of which responds to one of three basic needs. To respond to the need for efficiency around the basics, there is a stability pillar. To respond to the need for regular innovation, there is an entrepreneurial pillar. And to respond to the need for avoiding calcification, there is a habit-breaking pillar" (p. 315).
(Apollo balanced by Zeus and Athena?)

This last quotation emphasizes that the good American companies are not all Zeus, Athena, and Dionysus. Apollo is essential to stability and control. So are other things, as Peters and Waterman stress. Successful businesses know their markets; they keep to what they do well; and they emphasize their corporate values, so that everyone should, as in Japan, feel proud to be on board. The point is that they do not try to run an enlightened all-Apollonian organization but to keep it alive, kicking and changing by a liberal infusion of the other gods, who are more in tune with the American character.

Other studies agree. Rosabeth Moss Kanter also looked at leading American corporations to see how they coped with innovation. She found clear differences between what she called *segmentalized* companies, which put everything into separate bits or divisions and had tall hierarchies and an abundance of formal systems, and the more *integrative* companies, which are flatter and more open in their structure, don't rest on the laurels of past achievement, but adopt the future as a challenge and meet it with teams and entrepreneurs. She described one of the best of them as follows:

Chipco

"Employees portrayed Chipco (a pseudonym for a real and very successful company) with a variety of vivid images: a family, a competing guild, a society on a Pacific island, a group of people with an organisation chart hung around it, a gypsy society, a university, a theocracy, twenty-five different companies, and a company with ten thousand entrepreneurs. Organisation charts drawn by Chipco people often resembled plates of spaghetti more than a conventional set of boxes. Such imagery described many of the striking features of Chipco: its large number of enterprising employees, their interdependence in a complex matrix organization, the emphasis on knowledge and teamwork, continuing vibrant growth and change, and Chipco's sense of its own uniqueness as a market pioneer with a culture of creativity. Its youthful exuberance was aided by a workforce with a mean age under thirty."[8]

A place made for Athenians and Dionysians, with the odd Zeus.

When Apollonian organizations tried to innovate by doing it the Apollonian way—splitting up the task among the appropriate roles and divisions—nothing much happened. Although Apollo is necessary, in America at least, the energy and the charge come from the other gods.

There are, it seems, many more ways than one to run a successful organization. The gods can be balanced in different ways, and that balance can and should be affected by the surrounding culture. This, as we shall see, is an increasing problem in Western societies, where Apollo is not the most popular god but is still the preferred god of many organizations.

The Gods in Schools

Because of their setting, schools and other academic institutions are faced with a tug of war between Dionysus and Apollo, with Zeus as umpire. Their staff, the teachers or professors, are by training and inclination the members of a profession. They have, most of them, taken on board those professional values that pertain to service to the client, commitment to the profession, and the right to use their discretion in their job. Once admitted to a profession, the new professional is his or her own boss. Management, as we saw in Chapter 1, is the servant, not the master, of professionals, who are the true Dionysians.

To a teacher, the point of the work is the time spent with the students, usually on one's own, teaching them and working with them in one's own way, although within an agreed curriculum and timetable. If the classroom is no longer alluring, the job has lost its point. Teachers are therefore, by profession, likely to be Dionysian in their attitudes toward management and organization. On the other hand, when sitting in a classroom in front of twenty-five or more students, there is great incentive to turn from Dionysus to Zeus, when all is more or less under your control. On the other hand again, teachers are realistic enough to appreciate that they are working in an institution that must be formally managed. There must be institutional rules and procedures, meetings to go to, forms to be filled in, superiors and subordinates as well as colleagues. Apollo, in other words, must be acknowledged as a part of the institutional reality, however much it interferes with professional freedom and discretion.

Teachers, like most Dionysians who find themselves inside organizations, are, on the whole, ready to compromise by turning Athenian when their individual talents are harnessed to an institutional task by the group. Unfortunately, most schools, colleges, or universities are not in fact organized on Athenian lines, with the exception of some small nursery or primary schools and some special schools. The result is inevitably a clash of gods as Zeus and Apollo seek to manage Dionysus.

The clash is all the greater because schools tend not to be organized as professional institutions, in which management is the servant, but as producing organizations like businesses, in which management directs and controls. In Britain, one of the senior teachers is appointed head and in that capacity is seen as the manager of the school, not the servant of its professionals. In Britain, the secondary school is forced to operate against the grain of its culture, to be run like a factory rather than a professional office.

Who or What Are the Children?

Mingling in the staff room before I started the formal interviews of my research into school organization, I would ask the teachers I met how many people there were in the organization. Almost always I was give answers like 70 or 82 or 57. These were large comprehensive secondary schools with 1,200 or more students, but the teachers, when asked about the size of the organization, had instinctively left out the children. This did not mean they did not care about the children—most of them cared passionately—but they did not see them as fellow members of the organization: as clients, maybe, or as products?

It is the same in hospitals, I reflected, and in prisons. The temporary population of patients or prisoners is not seen as members of the organization but as something else. It makes a huge difference. If they are clients, their wants as well as their needs will be important. They will be seen as the judges of the performance of the institution and often of its individuals. They will be listened to as well as cared for. If, however, they are the products of the organization, they will be processed rather than served and have things done to them rather than for them. If the client image dominates, it will be the institution's fault if the examination is failed or the disease uncured. If the product model is dominant, the child will be judged to be at fault, the patient will be too ill to be treated successfully, or the prisoner will be unrepentant.

Dionysians have clients. Apollonians prefer products.

The children in primary schools have it better. In Britain they sit around tables, not in rows. They work on both individual and group tasks, talk among themselves, help one another, use one another. They stay for most of the day in the same place, leaving it only for special activities like physical education. They have the same teacher, or "boss," for most of the week. It is like working in the real world.

Secondary schools are different. At their most traditional the students work for ten bosses in one week in ten different locations, with perhaps three or more different work groups. They have no workplace to call their own, are forbidden to help others or to accept help, are discouraged from talking, are asked to memorize data rather than look them up, and are eventually tested by a procedure that will ensure that only a certain percentage passes. It is like a workplace only if the students are seen as products going through a factory, with a rigorous quality control procedure, not as workers in that factory.

Not all schools are like that, of course. More and more are finding ways to allow students to learn by working together on tasks, to use colleagues and resources, and to see the teacher as a counselor and coach rather than as a controller.

The dilemma for schools is that although they are quite properly staffed by Dionysian-leaning professionals, the size and complexity of their job drive them toward an Apollo-type structure, which is the logical route to efficiency. Carried too far, the Apollonian culture turns the school into a processing machine, with the kids as its products. The tendency then is to top it all off with a Zeus-like head who institutes, controls, and directs the Apollo structure—in a very un-Japanese way. You can hardly blame the head, whose only experience of managing others is likely to have been in a classroom where Zeus behavior is not out of place and comes naturally to many Dionysians. The end result, however, can be a cultural mixup that does little good to anyone.

Primary schools have evolved differently. Smaller sizes, less segmented tasks, and simpler structures have made it possible for the teachers to work together as one group while still retaining their individual areas of expertise. Some seem to operate as simple Athenian task cultures. Others are small enough to allow the head to operate very effectively as Zeus, forming the teachers and the children into a club around himself or herself. Given a good Zeus, who allows others to develop their own strengths, this is a perfectly viable model, but not every Zeus, alas, is a good Zeus.

To be culturally compatible, the secondary school has to think of itself as more like a professional partnership than a factory. Professional partnerships group individuals in teams; the Apollo element is essential but subservient; the organization is flat (there are often only three steps to the top status level), is led rather than managed with a maximum of consultation, and leaves as much room as possible for individual discretion. American schools, by separating the administrative element under a nonteacher, have gone some way down this path. British schools need to do something similar, as well as dividing themselves up into minischools in order to reduce their size.

Interestingly, as we shall see, the cultural dilemma of the school turns out to be no different from that faced by other organizations—the crisis of Apollo. Perhaps the answers will be the same.

The Gods among the Volunteers

Nonprofit organizations, be they churches, relief organizations, campaigning groups, or mutual-help bodies, always stoutly maintain that they are different from the organizations of business and government and have nothing to learn from them about management—a word that they dislike because of its overtones of direction and control, of manipulation and profit making. The truth is that they dislike the Apollonian culture, which they see as typical of business and government, preferring an often anarchic blend of Zeus and Dionysus, gathered together by Athenian groups sitting as committees or task groups.

At first sight, nonprofit organizations are composed of Dionysians, people who are there, as volunteers, because they want to be there making their contribution and doing their thing. The organization has no power or hold over them and therefore has to see its role as facilitating them and servicing their activities. The paid staff are presumably there to support, coordinate, and assist the volunteers, as it would be in a professional partnership.

It is not, however, as simple as that. Although the volunteers may indeed look for a Dionysian culture, they are not usually educated and licensed to act independently as is an architect or a doctor. Sometimes they are, as in the organizations that provide professional but volunteer counseling and advice, but in many organizations the volunteers are the fund-raisers and the leaflet folders, the unpaid hired help, with the true professionals being the salaried staff of the agency. It would not be, or feel, appropriate for the professional salaried staff to behave as the facilitators of the volunteer help—in a Dionysian way—yet it is also inappropriate to regard the volunteers as if they were normal employees of an Apollonian role culture.

It becomes even more complicated when one considers the congregation of a church. Are the members of that congregation part of the organization or its customers? Can they be organized, or are they there to be ministered to? Clearly they are not employees, so Apollonian procedures would be inappropriate, but what are they? It is the same with campaigning organizations, be they for peace, against famine, or in support of conservation. How are the volunteers to be classified? Are they workers or just followers?

It is because many volunteer organizations are unclear about these relationships that they have difficulty knowing what sort of organizational model they should use. How should they manage themselves? If Apollo is inappropriate, which god should they follow?

Nonprofit organizations can be of three types, each needing a different blend of the gods. It is when the types become confused or combined that the problems arise, although it needs to be emphasized that volunteer groups arc always harder to run well than are more ordinary organizations. The three types are fellowship, service, and campaigning.

Fellowship organizations are those that gather people together for mutual support, encouragement, and enjoyment. They include mutual-help groups, like single-parent families, as well as church congregations, social groups, and youth clubs. Such organizations welcome all who qualify and wish to be members. There is no selection: All single parents are welcome to a single-parent group, not just the best or the most competent, and all who "profess and call themselves Christians" are welcomed to their local church or chapel. The organizing required—no one would dream of calling it management—pertains to the provision of facilities and the structure of the occasions that are the focus of the fellowship. Much of the organizing is done by volunteer helpers, who see themselves as helpers or arrangers, not as managers or as persons in authority. Fellowship organizations, in fact, are quite Dionysian in the way they look at organizing: It is something done to facilitate the work of others.

Many nonprofit organizations start life in the fellowship mode but move into a *service* mode when they realize that more needs to be done for their membership than providing opportunities to meet together. There normally are specific needs to be met and specific forms of assistance or advice to be given. Service organizations do, however, have to be particular about whom they use to provide the advice or give the service; that is, anyone who volunteers is not necessarily good enough. As they become more service oriented, they tend to employ more paid staff and to insist on the proper selection and training of staff and volunteers. Professional standards must, after all, be applied. Goodwill is not enough. Service organizations, therefore, are the source of the apparent paradox, that the biggest and best of volunteer and charitable organizations are staffed by paid and professional staff. The volunteer element is found in the supervisory board or management committee, which represents the constituency being served, and often in the fund-raising effort that sustains the organization, although many such service organizations draw the bulk of their support from government or local authorities. Service organizations, therefore, are much more like other organizations: They need to be managed, directed, and controlled. They understand budgets, procedures, and defined roles as well as the nature of formal authority. They need Apollo as well as a bit of Zeus and Athena. The problem comes when the fellowship traditions and the service needs clash.

Third, a nonprofit organization can be a *campaigning* organization seeking to raise money for a cause; to combat injustice, poverty, or racism; or to fight for peace, individual rights, or better housing. Such organizations are different again. They welcome any adherents to their cause and are led rather than managed, although they also need an effective administrative backup to do research, organize meetings, or arrange recruitment drives. At their head there is usually a Zeus figure, for such organizations require a very personal and forceful form of leadership, a person who can represent and articulate what the movement stands for, and it is a movement rather than a formal organization.

Most nonprofit organizations end up as a mix of the three, although they may have started off at either the fellowship or the campaigning end. That is perhaps a natural and understandable progression, but it leaves the resulting organization with three conflicting cultures. The theory of cultural propriety can end up as a battleground for the gods in many volunteer headquarters, as Apollo seeks to apply some order to a Dionysian tradition infiltrated by Zeus. Athena is often seen as the way out, with her emphasis on the group rather than on hierarchy, and on professionalism in the pursuit of a solution. But Athenian organizations, as we have seen, are unstable cultures, hard to manage effectively, and they can be expensive. They easily drift into more committees, more project groups, which connive to perpetuate themselves, more independent cells doing their own thing. Athena, undisciplined, reverts to Apollo or Zeus, and so it often is with the volunteer world.

The Confusions of a Nonprofit Organization

The organization was founded nearly one hundred years ago. Its aims were clear—to provide a meeting place for lonely strangers in our big cities.

That was easy enough, but the organization felt that more needed to be done for particular groups. Some needed help with accommodation; others wanted advice on jobs or counseling, legal assistance, or just money. Gradually, the organization set up separate agencies to provide each of these services. What had started as a fellowship organization run by volunteers had evolved into a service agency, staffed by professionals and funded by volunteers, but the old fellowship ethos remained, which said that everyone who was a stranger could belong and that every volunteer had the right to help.

It went further than that, as the organization began to perceive that it might be more effective to campaign to get rid of injustices rather than patching up the aftereffects. So a campaigning wing was added to the organization, taking a radical stand for individual rights and becoming politically active under a forceful leader.

The new director wanted to bring order to the situation. She set out to introduce some management discipline, with objectives, budgets, performance reviews, and personnel appraisals. The fellowship strand, which still permeated the organization and was well represented on its many committees, was outraged. Such techniques, they said, were quite inappropriate to the "open house, everyone welcome, contribute what you can" philosophy for which the organization stood. "Not so," said the service agency groups. "We are nowadays in competition with many other organizations who offer similar services. We need to be more efficient, tougher, and more discriminating." The campaigning arm took no notice—there were more important causes, and the leader had his own band of enthusiasts who welcomed any adherent to their cause. It seemed, reflected the director, as if there were really three quite different organizations jostling together under one roof, making living together difficult.

Or three gods in one setting.

The Gods in Church

Many church congregations have in the best Christian tradition, proclaimed their task to be the threefold one of worship, ministry, and prophecy. All three are necessary to provide proper witness to a Christian presence in that place. What the congregation often fails to realize is that each task implies a different (Greek) god. Worship is akin to fellowship, ministry to services, and prophecy to campaigning. There are therefore really three different organizations needed, all under one umbrella. It can be done. The gods can learn to live together, as Chapter 3 demonstrated, but often it is one god who triumphs over the rest, so that in the end only one of the tasks is properly done. It is perhaps unfortunate that the servant tradition is taken so literally to heart by many churches, because that best fits the Dionysian tradition and the fellowship model, meaning that the tasks of ministry and prophecy are inadequately done. Organizationally, it is probable that many congregations will end up as little more than holy huddles.

Fifty-seven Varieties

Japan and America, schools and charities—these are but four of many possible settings. Hospitals and prisons, armies and parliaments, Mexico and Nigeria—they all demand different cultural blends in their organizations. The theory of cultural propriety must take account of the surroundings. It would, however, be unfortunate if every setting felt that it had to work out its own unique theory of management, not heeding what the rest may be up to. Wheels come in different sizes, materials, and colors, but the principle need not be reinvented each time.

Organizations can and should learn from one another, which is not the same as saying that they should copy one another. The gods can be blended in different ways, but they each represent continuing traditions that seem to apply to a range of contexts and settings. The Japanese may find it easier, culturally, to run Apollo organizations, but they put a lot of effort and ingenuity into the task as well. We can learn from that, just as we can learn from the best American businesses and the best schools and charities.

II

THE APOLLONIAN
CRISIS

5

The Dilemma
of Apollo

The first part of this book may have made things look easy. They
are not, of course. It has always been easier to describe principles
than to follow them, which is why grandparents, who no longer
have to practice what they preach, have such a good time. Management, it should by now have become clear, is the art of combining opposites, of blending the cultures, or of managing paradox. One set of pressures drives one toward tight control, central
monitoring, keeping it all at one's fingertips while at the very
same time there are many instincts and very valid reasons for
doing just the opposite, decentralizing, delegating, and letting
go. Management is the art of compromise.

Part II explores the ways in which the pull of opposites has
come to a head in Western organizations. The pressures to become more Apollonian, to make organizations tidier and more
formal, are pressing and convincing, but so are the opposing
pressures to recognize the individuals who make up those organizations and the need to give them more scope, more rights, and
more independence. I will argue in this second part that these
more individualist, or Dionysian, pressures, which spring from a
freer and richer society, are inexorable. Apollo must compromise. The result will be new kinds of organizations, new structures, and new ways of relating individuals to organizations. It

Negative Power

adds up to an organizational revolution that will affect not only the way we manage our institutions but also the way we live and plan our lives. Nor is it that far off. There are signs enough to suggest that the year 2000 will see the waning of the employment society as we have known it.

The Drift to Apollo

If you are sitting near the top of an organization, responsible in whole or in part for its continued success, or at least survival, there is a strong urge to want to make it bigger and more internally consistent. There are good reasons for each of these tendencies, which need owe nothing to the supposed egos, lust for power, or dictatorial ambitions of those in authority.

First, bigness. The bigger you are, the more able you are to influence you own destiny. A small organization has to ask others for money: banks, other lenders, the stock market, the government. The more money you, as manager, can generate internally, the less you will be dependent on others, and if and when you need their money, the more likely they are to believe your estimates of your future.[1] The bigger, therefore, the easier.

And bigness brings clout: clout in the marketplace, enabling one to offer comprehensive ranges or services or to launch sales drives, price offensives, or massive advertising campaigns; clout in the research laboratories, allowing adequate finance for adequate research and development, all of which is insurance against the future (93 percent of the research in Britain happens in large—more than three thousand—firms); clout in recruitment, offering scope for varied careers within the protection of one organization.

And finally, bigness brings flexibility and a built-in insurance. A loss in one area can be offset by unusual profits elsewhere. Resources can be taken from one use and given to another without the need for anyone outside to know or be concerned. It is no accident that the big corporations are private universes, revealing only the tips of their icebergs to their shareholders in their balance sheets or to their employees in their internal communications. Privacy carries its freedoms, and as the custodians of the organization's future, its managers and directors understandably want as much discretion as they can retain and bigness to provide that discretion.

Why Do Firms Grow?

S. J. Prais analyzed the evolution of giant firms in Britain.[2] He pointed out that the share of net output contributed by the one hundred largest manufacturing firms in Britain rose from 16 percent in 1900 to 22 percent in 1949 and to 41 percent in 1970. But even though the size of the firms increased, the size of the plants remained relatively static. Prais argues that it is economics in marketing, transport, and the likelihood of cheaper finance that encourage growth, not economies of scale at the plant level.

Does it work?

Leslie Hannah and John Kay agree that although firms grow, plants remain small, but they found little evidence that the new giants performed better.[3] The giants certainly export less and have higher labor costs than the overall average firm does.

In search of the "clout" of size, have we lost efficiency?

Why Have Large Schools?

Schools with 2,000 pupils seem excessively large to some. Why were they designed like that? Well, it is logical, really. Suppose you want to offer a minimum choice of twelve subjects to be taught in the sixth grade, with an average of ten students per class. If each student takes three courses, that gives you a sixth grade class of 360 students and 180 in each of the two years of the sixth grade. If half of each class leaves at age sixteen, the end of compulsory schooling, you will need an average class size of 360 to produce your sixth grade. If they join the school at eleven, there will be five years of 360 students and two of 180, which works out at 2,160. Two thousand then seems a rather modest target.

The logic is impeccable, given the assumptions. But are the assumptions inevitable? Should schools cover an age range from eleven to eighteen? If the students drop out at age sixteen, the arguments break down. If they started at thirteen, the school would be significantly smaller. If a higher percentage stayed on, the school size could be proportionately reduced. And so on.

Given the logic, however, and the assumptions, size is inevitable, and so, therefore, is Apollo.

The second urge is toward *consistency*. Consistency is desirable to a manager for two reasons. If the future is consistent with one's expectations of it, then planning can be tighter, and all the provisions for that future can be taken care of—in that way things will happen as they were expected to happen. A catering firm once claimed that the *predictability* of its operations was such that it could forecast to within two dozen the number of eggs that would be consumed by its 250 London outlets in any given day. This consistency over time allowed it to run a more cost effective pur chasing and delivery system than its competitors could.

Most organizations seek to achieve *consistency of predictability* by choosing the kind of future they want and then setting out to achieve it. That is not quite the way they put it, of course. They talk instead of forecasts, long-term plans, and corporate objectives, but essentially these plans are intended to be self-fulfilling prophecies. J. K. Galbraith, an American economist, found alarming portents in the ability of large corporations to create self-fulfilling prophecies, seeing this as a corruption of democracy. Others have deplored the way that the consumer becomes just a part of the corporation's plans, the patient an "input" to the hospital's operations. We need not, at this stage, take sides on the rights and wrongs of this managerial urge for predictability but take the complaints only as evidence of its existence.

Managerially, consistency over time, or predictability, is highly desirable. The longer one can guarantee predictability, the more scope there is for tightening up the operational side of the organization. Consistency over time is an entirely normal and appropriate instinct for those seeking managerial comfort.

Unpredictability at Home

Have you ever stayed in an unpredictable household?

"Is there anything for supper?"

"How should I know, have a look. There may be if the

children haven't eaten it all. There isn't anything? Well, don't blame me, I've had other things to do."

"Where's Alan, we've got to leave now?"
"He's gone off on his bike."
"Did he say when he'd be back?"
"No idea."

"I need the car today, dear."
"You can't have it, I'm afraid, I have to drive out and meet a client in Westchester."
"Well, then, how am I supposed to get to mother's?"

For a time, the feeling of spontaneity carries its own brand of charm. On a holiday, the charm can linger for days, even weeks. But slowly the irritation and its costs mount. It is impossible to plan under these conditions. Time is wasted as people stand around. Activities cannot be coordinated or days organized in advance. Every joint venture becomes a major event. Instead of everyone doing his or her own thing, everyone begins to feel thwarted by the others. Tempers flare. Stress mounts.
Organizations demand predictability.

Consistency across activities, or *comparability*, is also highly desirable. In any case, it is pressed on us in organizations whether we want it or not.

Comparability is desirable, even essential, for the *dovetailing* that lies at the heart of most organizational activities. One task depends on another and contributes to another. Seen at its most obvious in the automated assembly line, the principle of dovetailing applies to the accounts department and the dispatch warehouse as much as to the factory.

Comparability is necessary for *control* from the top. Without a proper basis for comparison, control becomes arbitrary, governed more by whims and impulses than by rationality.

Comparability is imperative in certain *work flows*, particularly the copy or flow types. The arrival of new expensive technology that demands a quick turnaround to justify its existence drives organizations to flow or copy work patterns and the consistency or comparability that these demand. The high technology of process industries is one example of a technology that demands a precise standard of consistency between inputs in order to operate efficiently. More commonly, the computer, with its insatiable appetite for input data, has imposed copy conditions across organizations that did not need them or want them.

Consistency is also forced on organizations from outside. The legislation, government regulations, and union bargaining mechanisms all encourage consistency, a comparability across activities. In some organizations, this consistency is achieved initially through *centralization:* for instance, by establishing a central negotiating office to deal with union negotiations. But centralization is only one way, and can be the most costly, to achieve the consistency that is often the driving force behind the apparent need to centralize.

There are, then, these twin pressures toward bigness and consistency. They are not only understandable but, viewed from the standpoint of operational efficiency, much to be desired. In the original sense of the word, things are more "manageable" if they are under control. Both bigness and consistency increase control. Not surprisingly, ambitious managers concentrate their attention on opportunities for growth and on improved systems of control.

However, both bigness and consistency imply an Apollonian culture. Size, as we showed in an earlier chapter, brings formality, impersonality, and rules and procedures in its train. There is no way out of it. When someone cannot rule by glance of eye and word of mouth because there are just too many people, he has to lean on formal systems of hierarchy, information, and control. Similarly, consistency implies budgets, forms, standardized methods, fixed reporting periods, common documents, and the whole barrage of bureaucracy. The ineluctable logic of efficiency drives organizations toward Apollo and the role culture.

Apollo Triumphant

It has been suggested that by the end of the century, fewer than two hundred companies will control more than 70 percent of private-sector activity in the Western democracies. In Britain, the one hundred largest manufacturing companies accounted for 22 percent of total net output in 1949, but 48 percent in 1990.

Research by John Child of Aston University shows that in the faster-growing and more profitable large companies, as total size increases, so do certain types of systems and procedures: sophisticated financial controls applied to a wide range of activities, a precise definition of operative tasks by management, the application of work study and methods, the use of labor turnover statistics, the planning of recruitment, and the regular updating of company forms and documents.

Apollo thrives on size.

The Resistance to Apollo

Unfortunately, logic no longer reigns supreme. Psychology also counts, and Apollonian systems are managed and worked by humans. And from these humans comes an increasing resistance to the inexorable advance of the Apollonian culture. One strand of this resistance suggests that we are creating systems that are simply too complex to be managed by humans, that logic has outdistanced psychological capacity.

A second strand argues that the extreme specialization of the work role is alienating, that it deprives people of control over their destiny and separates their work from their other lives: family, recreation, community.

A third strand says that rightly or wrongly, the new norms and values of society expressed through our schools and traditions of child rearing do not encourage the kind of obedience and subordination to imposed methods that are required by Apollonian organizations.

The First Strand of Resistance

Size brings complexity, and it may well be that in the time available we humans cannot handle the complex decisions of the mammoth corporations. Professor Elliott Jaques believes that people of immense conceptual span are needed and that there are too few of these in any generation. The evidence of mergers has been that bigness on its own does not lead to increased efficiency but, rather, the reverse as we import more administrative "slack" to handle the increased complexity. Computers have immeasurably increased our capacity to handle information and complexity, but they have also added hugely to the information that we must handle. Some multinationals, looking at the incredible complexity of trying to manage a wide range of national subsidiaries in a constantly shifting environment, have, in a sense, abandoned the pursuit of "the one best" solution and left their subsidiaries to go their own way. Most managers would agree that the apparent logical pull of bigness and consistency does not seem to make their job any easier.

A cultural analysis based on patron gods would suggest why. The Apollonian culture demanded by bigness and consistency works as long as the work is routine, the environment is stable, and change is infrequent. Unfortunately, as an organization grows larger, it imports uncertainty when it becomes involved with more and more outside groups and is exposed to a wider range of forces. Ironically, as an organization grows larger, it ought to attempt to make do with less of Apollo's culture rather than more. This is the first glance at the Apollonian paradox: the tendency for Apollo to self-destruct. For just as size creates an internal need for Apollonian methods, so the very increase in that culture tends to make the total organization less responsive to its environment, less capable of changing, more dinosaurlike than ever—impressive but out of touch and often out of control.

The first consequence of the excessive complexity of large Apollonian systems is what Derek Sheane of ICI called the "symptomology of bureaucratic breakdown."[4] His list of symptoms includes

1. The invisible decision: No one knows how or where decisions are made.
2. Unfinished business: Too many tasks are started but not finished.
3. Coordination paralysis: Nothing can be done without checking with a host of other interconnected units.
4. Nothing new: Bureaucracies polish but do not invent. This applies to both processes and products.
5. Pseudoproblems: Bureaucracies seem to magnify some is-

sues until they become an internal organizational epidemic, for no apparent reason.

6. Embattled center: The conflicts between the center and the local or regional units increase as the center battles for consistency.

7. Negative deadlines: The dates for reports and historical explanations become more important than doing the work. He who carries bad news is given priority over those who bring good news.

8. In-tray domination: Individuals react to their inputs rather than impose their own initiatives.

The Costs of Waiting

Specialization should make things change, but the costs of coordinating specialized activities can outweigh the savings by far.

Take batch production.

The component to be manufactured is pared down to a set of operations on machine tools. There may be as many as twenty separate operations. Each operation requires a different tool or at least a different setting of the same tool. In between operations, the component has to wait. It has been calculated that out of the average one hundred days that it takes a component to go through a normal efficient factory, it spends ninety-nine days just waiting.[5] The cost in work-in-progress can be huge if the material of the component is expensive.

In the name of consistency, we specialize, then we coordinate, and so we pay.

The second consequence of excessive complexity is that the burden of holding the thing together now falls on the manager— typically the middle manager. In a straightforward Apollonian role culture, he would be an ordinary man in a straightforward routine administrative job. Instead, today, in the oversized organization, he receives all the imported *uncertainty* yet is equipped only with the (Apollonian) methods for dealing with *certainty*. Restrained by the rules and procedures dictated by the pressures for consistency, he must find a way of coping with the inconsistent. He can do it, Zeus-like, only by ignoring the rules and procedures, by playing organizational politics, by taking organizational risks, and by working enormously hard. Many succeed in doing this, but the costs can be high, both to themselves and to their organizations. It is understandable if they feel under-rewarded in a society that depends on the organizations that they seem to be carrying on their shoulders.

The cost of coping with imported uncertainty in an Apollonian system designed for certainty is overload. When the overload gets too large, ways of coping with it must be devised. All these "coping mechanisms," in effect, create "slack" or inefficiency in the organization.

Coping with Overload

Think of yourself when tired, when there is more to do than you can easily cope with.

Do you ever

Polarize: Push problems into extremes of black or white, good or bad? Do you find yourself saying to a subordinate, "I don't want to know that there are pros and cons, I want to know whether it is viable or not." (It is easier to decide between black and white than shades of gray.)

Shorten Time Horizons: Put off to tomorrow what does not have to be done today; leave the five-year plan until the week after next; think about the growing apathy over the Christmas holidays. (Postponement of longer-term decisions is one way to lessen the load.)

Search for Routines: Say, "What did we do last time?" or "PO requirement," even if the situation doesn't neatly fit that box? (Finding a routine avoids a decision.)

Delight in Trivia: When baffled, turn your attention to an easy problem or delve into some issue of minor importance. (Taking the easy things first does at least reduce the load.)

React, not Proact: Deal with the in-tray before going out to change the world, or cope with events as they arrive rather than seek to influence them before they arrive. (Reactivity reduces the list of things to be done; pro-activity adds to it.)

Flare Up: Show irritation, anger, or emotion over matters of relatively minor importance, often to illustrate that you are still around and matter. (Emotion acts as a relief valve.)

Withdraw: Either physically or emotionally, take yourself away from the center of action—shut yourself in your office, go on a trip, or claim that "it's all unimportant anyway." (Withdrawal puts the load into a reduced perspective.)

Hammer Away: Do what you normally do, only more of it. Work longer and harder, write more reports, hold more committees, or make more visits. (More effort will reduce the load.)

Escape: Into excess behavior, often accompanied by unnecessary humor, drink, drugs, or the like. (These are forms of sublimation.)

Break Down: Collapse, usually into a hospital. (An extreme form of enforced withdrawal.)

All these mechanisms do cope with the overload, for you. But they either export it to someone else or they reduce the ultimate efficiency or success of the operation. Some of them (*Escape* and *Breakdown*) have unwanted consequences for oneself.

The Second Strand of Resistance

The second strand of resistance to Apollo arises from the emphasis of the Apollonian culture of management on the "role," as distinct from the "individual." Here lie the ideas of "organizational sin" and "corporate slavery."

We have already noted that traditionally "sin" meant "denying oneself," being false, in word or deed or thought, to one's true beliefs and true self. The concept of sin has these days been so downgraded to a list of mere peccadilloes that it is even socially respectable to boast, "I am a confirmed sinner," but one would still be unlikely to boast, "I do not believe in what I do, nor does my behavior reveal the kind of person I am." That is simply not a boast. Instead it is a kind of bleat, and it is heard often enough. A man's job or official role can become his private crucifixion when in order to do his job, he finds himself forced to act and speak in ways that do not reflect his real beliefs.

George Orwell described how once, as a minor colonial official in Burma, he found himself—an apostle of nonviolence and a lover of living things—raising a gun to kill a harmless elephant because he lacked the will, or perhaps the courage, to deny the demands of what others called his "duty." It is a moving description of a private shame, or sin.

For many people, organizations seem to reek of this kind of private sin. It is not that employees are forced to cheat, or bribe, or lie—although such dishonesties are not unknown in organizations—but in smaller ways they feel pushed to submerge their identity in the job, argue cases of whose merit they are not convinced, give priority to rituals they know to be charades, be charming to those they despise, appear fierce when they feel sympathy, and act committed when unconvinced. Perhaps it is not profit that makes youth shy away from organizations—but sin?

The idea that organizations deprive people of the right to express their values and their personalities in their work has a long and distinguished pedigree. William Morris and D. H. Lawrence in England, Henry Thoreau and Herbert Marcuse in America, Bertolt Brecht in Germany, Simone Weil and André Malraux in France, and, of course, Karl Marx all have sung this song. The IBM young men are but the latest exponents of the idea, which is embedded in many Western cultures.

Three Quotations

Karl Marx
"In his work, therefore, [the worker] does not affirm himself but denies himself . . . does not develop freely his physical and mental energy but mortifies his body and ruins his mind. . . . His labour is . . . not voluntary but coerced; it is forced labour. It is therefore not the satisfaction of a need: it is merely a means to satisfy needs external to it."

Frederick Taylor
(the originator of "scientific management"): "One of the very first requirements for a man who is fit to handle pig iron as a regular occupation is that he shall be so stupid and so phlegmatic that he more nearly resembles an ox than any other type."

Adam Smith
"The man whose life is spent in performing simple operations . . . has no occasion to exert his understanding. . . . He generally becomes as stupid and ignorant as it is possible for a human creature to become."

Runaway Slaves

Not long ago, IBM France had a new experience: It lost a team of software specialists, who decided to leave to found a business of their own. The manager of Computer Services, the new company, observed, "Never has man owed more to a private business enterprise. Without IBM, the economic level of our planet would not be what it is today. Why, then, did we quit? To perform more interesting work, and above all for moral reasons. Tomorrow, the real power will belong to those who master software. Whereas this firm has dominated the world's information-processing market, the French engineers participating in IBM's activities have by no means been involved with decision making. They are in some ways nothing but 'golden slaves'."

All these people see Apollonian organizations as inevitably alienating places. Alan Fox demonstrated that low levels of discretion lead to low levels of trust. Apollonian organizations cannot tolerate much discretion—it would violate their consistency. They will not, cannot, be high-trust organizations. One can redesign jobs to allow marginally greater discretion, introduce flexitime or autonomous groups, or create works councils, but all these remain placebos, temporary pills to relieve the pain and alleviate the inherent incompatibility between man and this type of work. Today, more than 90 percent of the working population are in organizations, and many of them—the majority, probably—in a bureaucracy of one sort or another. One hundred years ago, fewer than 30 percent worked in any form of organization, and very few of those institutions that did exist would have been classified as bureaucratic, even if they had other flaws and faults. The bureaucratic phenomenon is, then, of fairly recent origin. Only today are we becoming aware of the extent of the malaise. When it afflicted only a minority, it could be ignored, or the minority could be regarded as volunteers, prepared to suffer the so-called indignities of organizational work because they wanted the money, the security, or the promise of higher status in time to come. Now that it is the majority that is involved, "sin" is no longer a voluntary option but a built-in requirement of life. In Apollonian organizations, the individual is a *role* more than a *person;* initiative comes from above, not from within; and creativity too often is counted as disruption.

Rules for Stifling Initiative

Rosabeth Kanter took the following ten rules for stifling initiative from her observations of "segmentalist" (Apollonian) companies in America:[6]

1. Regard any new idea from below with suspicion—because it is new and because it is from below.

2. Insist that people who need your approval to act first go through several other levels of management to get their signatures.

3. Ask departments or individuals to challenge and criticize each other's proposals. (That saves you the job of deciding: You just pick the survivor.)

4. Express your criticisms freely, and withhold your praise. (That keeps people on their toes.) Let them know they can be fired at any time.

5. Treat problems as signs of failure, to discourage people from letting you know when something in their area isn't working.

6. Control everything carefully, and make sure that people count anything that can be counted, frequently.

7. Make decisions to reorganize or change policies in secret and spring them on people unexpectedly. (That also keeps people on their toes.)

8. Make sure that any request for information is fully justified and that it isn't distributed too freely. (You don't want data to fall into the wrong hands.)

9. Assign to lower-level managers, in the name of delegation and participation, responsibility for figuring out how to cut back, lay off, or move people around.

10. Above all, never forget that you, the higher-ups, already know everything important about this business.

The Third Strand of Resistance

This problem is not concerned so much with rights and wrongs as with the way things are. A new generation has grown up in the Western democracies, a generation that is less frightened (it has experienced no major wars), is less hungry, less insecure, and perhaps less greedy than preceding generations. But not only have external conditions changed (improved?) for the new youth, so have the ways of rearing and educating children. Education is as much about the nature of authority as it is about information and skills. When the parents of the young currently in their twenties went to school, most of them sat in rows and copied down what the teacher said, only to write it back to him in due course as a test or examination. Whether or not this was an efficient method of learning, it certainly conveyed the message that the younger, or more junior, or less clever, did what their elders and betters said. The message from the home matched that of the school, that obedience and conformity to those in charge were a prerequisite of life. Today, it is different. My young children sit in groups in their school. They work on projects. They think of themselves as learning rather than being taught. They are encouraged to express their own personalities in stories, poems, and paintings, instead of memorizing or imitating those of the great. And again, for better or worse, the home mirrors the school. From an early age, due partly to the exigencies of small houses and communal living, the young are treated as equals in the family, with a right to their own views and attitudes. In adolescence, the new affluence, the increased ability to earn marginal income, allows the growing men and women to become rapidly independent of their elders. The result is predictable and was summed up in David Yankelovitch's survey:

Authority to the Young

David Yankelovitch carried out a survey for the IDR Third Fund to investigate the changing views of American student youth.[7] Among many other facets of their attitudes, he looked at the increasing resistance to authority and concluded that the greatest single erosion of relationship to authority is in the "boss" relationship and the work situation. In 1968, over half of all students (56 percent) did not mind the future prospect of being bossed around on the job. This number fell to 49 percent in 1969, 43 percent in 1970, and down to 36 percent in 1971. The result: Today, two out of three students do not easily see themselves submitting to the authority of a "boss."

A student's relationship to authority of all kinds—including a boss—is, at best, one of grudging but not easy acceptance. Students see the major barrier standing in the way of securing desirable work to be their attitude toward authority. No obstacle comes even close to this one, including political views, style of dress, or unwillingness to conform.

This random concatenation of words and phrases captures as well as any formal definition can the things that students do not want in their world.

Professional . . . system . . . planning for the future . . . conceptual framework . . . experiment . . . organization . . . detachment . . . management . . . verification . . . facts . . . technology . . . cost effectiveness . . . theory . . . rationalization . . . efficiency . . . measurement . . . statistical controls . . . manipulate . . . mechanization . . . institutions . . . power . . . determinism . . . intelligence testing . . . abstract thought . . . programming . . . calculate . . . objectivity . . . behaviorism . . . modification of the human environment . . . literal . . . molded to specification . . . genetic planning . . . achievement.

Dionysians all?

Yankelovitch's study was done in America in 1971. Nearly three decades later it would be interesting to know whether his subjects still felt the same now that they were in authority. It is easier to follow Dionysus when one is young and irresponsible!

British Views of Work

A survey by the *Guardian* newspaper tapped the satisfactions that people in work wanted from their job.

At the top of the list came personal freedom, the respect of people one worked with, learning something new, challenge, and completing a project. (Athenians all, with a touch of Dionysus).

Security came seventeenth in the list, working conditions twenty-first, with money, organization, and social status bringing up the rear. (Apollonians were much in the minority, although it might have been very different if the questions had been asked of people not in work but wanting it!)

In his book *Rethink,* Gordon Rattray Taylor called attention to the difference between what he terms *patrism* and *matrism* in our society. The values and attitudes of patrism might be called traditional, or tough, as opposed to radical, or tender. Patrism believes in order and discipline, wishes to maintain the traditions of the past and respect for authority; it values self-control and rational behavior, distinguishes male and female roles, and puts more faith in experience and age than in youth. Matrism, on the other hand, is optimistic about the future, decries the past, believes in openness and likes emotions, makes little distinction between the sexes, wants discussion rather than orders, places reliance on expertise rather than experience, and values youth and imagination more than age. Rattray Taylor is convinced that there is a marked swing toward matrism in our society.

In my cultural terms, we are bringing up the young in a Dionysian tradition—individuality and personal expression—with Athenian overtones—groups, projects, and shared values. It is not surprising that they then reject the Apollonian culture when they begin to meet it at work or that they look increasingly to the established professions for their careers (the schools of law and medicine are those in most demand in universities everywhere) or to the new professions in the media, writing, or design or fashion. These are the Dionysian occupations, and today they are overcrowded.

In some countries, Japan perhaps most obviously, the educational and family systems are still Apollonian. There the bureaucratic organization is more readily accepted, even welcomed as a natural and necessary part of life. In Germany, France, Switzerland, and parts of Italy, the Apollonian tradition in schools and homes is still strong but weakening. In these countries, the Apollonian culture is still viable and cost effective, but perhaps not for very much longer.

There is, in other words, a growing clash in Western society between organizational logic and the feelings of the individual. The argument that efficiency justifies the subordination of individualism to the organization may no longer carry so much weight in societies in which efficiency and (relative) abundance are taken for granted. Japan has demonstrated that there are ways of running Apollonian cultures that make them more tolerable to the individual as well as efficient, but as we shall see in later chapters, this is achieved for only a minority of the working population and at some cost to the remainder. We have also noted that what works in Japan may not work so well in countries in which the underlying culture gives a higher priority to individualism and risk or to personal power or feminism. The growing crisis of the Apollonian organization is likely to be most pressing in Western countries, but its pressures are likely to be felt everywhere, even in Japan, as more and more groups react against the overweening control of the organization. To help them in that reaction they have one powerful weapon—the organizational hijack.

The Fruits of Organization

To celebrate Queen Elizabeth II's Silver Jubilee in 1977, the *Readers Digest* compared conditions then with those at the start of her reign.

In 1952, the small family car cost the equivalent of 62½ weeks' work by the average industrial worker. Twenty-five years later, it needed only 32½ weeks, even though wages had more than doubled in the meantime.

Barcelona, by scheduled flight from London, cost 4¾ weeks' work at the beginning of the period, but only 1½ at the end of it.

Twenty-two minutes' work in 1977 was enough to buy a dozen eggs, compared with 57 minutes in 1952; 23 minutes for a pound of butter, instead of 32 minutes; and 11 minutes for a box of cornflakes, instead of 17½ minutes.

Even a bottle of Scotch, loaded with ever-increasing taxes, cost only 2¾ hours' work in the Silver Jubilee year, compared with 7¼ in 1952.

The fruits of Apollo? Could it have happened otherwise? Will it continue if Apollo is weakened?

Organizational Hijacks

This is how it works. Organizations are designed logically, according to the precepts of Apollo. As in a clock, each wheel fits the next in a hierarchical dovetailing of systems. One part depends on another and, in its own turn, is essential to the proper functioning of its neighbor. But take one cog out of a large clock and the whole apparatus will be halted. Clocks are not designed with alternative relief systems, because that would be an expensive and seldom-utilized form of slack for a mechanism that can count on its cogs always being there. But it is not so with organizations. The cogs cannot be relied on. Indeed, the power to stop or remove a cog is actually given to the cog itself. In organizational terms, the cog is a work group, a subassembly unit, a department. Should the members of these groups decide to withhold their labor, skill, or talent, they could bring a tightly designed organization to a halt.

In many organizations, this hijack capacity has been unwittingly handed to the very people who are most likely to be resistant to the Apollonian tradition. They may feel bruised as individuals, but into their hands has been thrust a weapon with which to hold their enemy for ransom. Increasingly they will use it, indulging in a walkout or a spontaneous strike, often in support of some trivial incident.

The incident itself can be merely the product, the symptom of a deeper discontent. The ministrike or walkout often fails to win the support of the union (which can perceive the longer-term consequences of supporting hijackers), or even of fellow workers whose earnings can cease if the whole system grinds to a halt. But in the short term, it will usually pay the organization to bribe the group back to work, even though the longer-term precedents are likely to be punitive in terms of higher rates across the board.

The monolithic, overtight design of our organizations is an invitation to hijack and a major contributory cause to wage inflation. We have given what is called *negative power* in huge amounts to those people most likely to use it. Apollonian cultures come equipped with this time bomb, which will destroy the whole temple if it is not defused.

Negative Power

In 1974, a Turkish Airlines DC-10 crashed north of Paris, killing more than three hundred people. A ground mechanic had failed to close the door of a luggage compartment in the appointed manner. He was probably the lowest-paid member of the ground staff. Reputedly, he was illiterate. Yet he had the power to destroy one of the most sophisticated and best cared-for of man's creations. He had little or no positive power, but immense negative power. In this case, he used it unintentionally. It can always be used intentionally.

All members of interlocking systems can find some negative power to use. Its conscious use, often by lower officials in bureaucracies, is a way of reminding themselves and the organization that they do exist and do matter. Negative power is therefore fertilized by unhappiness, low morale, or a feeling of powerlessness.

While traveling in India, I needed to rent a bedroll for an overnight train journey. This is a complicated procedure at the best of times, involving filling in a document with seven separate copies, so I allowed plenty of time. Neverthless, on arrival at the desk of the key functionary responsible for renting bedding, I was informed that he was closing the office for one hour for his statutory mealtime allowance. I pointed out that by the time he reopened, my train would have departed. He expressed regrets but assured me there would be a later train. I begged him—yes, begged him—to deal with my request before he closed the office, but he was adamant. His time was already overdue. Had he no assistant? "Not today, he is absent attending his sister's wedding." "Can I talk to your superior?" "He is not, alas, available until tomorrow morning." "Would this [showing some money] help?" "Ah, no, sir, I'm not that sort of man, sir." By this time, we had used up more time than the actual issue of the bedding could conceivably have required. The desire to exercise his negative power, for whatever reason, prevailed over logic, economics, and human charity. I spent a very uncomfortable night.

Less perceived, less dramatic, but more pervasive than the active use of negative power to hijack organizations is the stealthy threat of *absenteeism.* So stealthy is this threat that figures are hard to collect, even in statistics-conscious Britain. Some estimates, however, suggest that absence due to sickness, family need, or just unexplained, is as much as one hundred times greater in Britain than days lost through strikes. This silent stilling of the clock is the real threat to Apollonian cultures. It is countered by overemployment, by sufficient overmanning to cope with any anticipated absenteeism, by manpower slack. But this remedy exacerbates the disease. If it is obvious that you are not needed, you may all the more easily be absent. And the cost? Immense. Here is the "concealed unemployment" in industry; here is the true nature of the "English disease." Maybe it is not after all a disinclination to work but a silent expression of negative power in reaction against the Apollonian cultures of organizations that saps the energy of Britain's productive machines. And the disease is not confined to Britain. It is estimated that the net average working day (after sickness, absenteeism, and holidays) of the Italian worker is only four hours (instead of the formal eight), whereas Swedes each take an average of twenty-four days a year on sick leave.

National Negative Power

Mancur Olson wrote a book with the impressive title *The Rise and Decline of Nations.*[8] It is important but depressing. In it, he argues that a society that has stayed politically stable for many years with unchanged boundaries (Britain? America?) tends to accumulate all sorts of collective organizations and informal collusions. The most effective of these are small groups with narrow but identical interests. These coalitions find that they have more to gain by diverting more of the nation's resources to themselves or their causes than by trying to increase the total of all the resources. Distribution, not creation, is the name of their game. They are exclusive; new members mean less for the old members; they resist innovation in order to protect their own markets or constituencies; they slow down change; and they make political life more divisive. Trade unions are one of these coalitions, but more important are cartels, trade associations, and professional bodies.

Wars, revolutions, and changed boundaries disrupt these conditions. Turbulence, therefore, with the prospect of a more stable future, is the likeliest predictor of economic success, because it destroys, for a time, the possibility of negative power.

Overcoming the Resistance

If the efficiency of Apollo is to triumph, the resistance to it must be overcome. We have identified three strands to this resistance, and now we must examine counters to each. How effective these counters may be is a question to which we will continually return while we consider them.

The first strand had to do with the unmanageability of the complexity of large Apollonian structures. But perhaps we should not accept defeat: Can't we increase the comprehension span of selected individuals and equip them with further computational aids? Already the computer is in the boardroom. There are programs that can evaluate the likely outcomes of any combination of strategic decisions and flash them almost instantaneously on screens in front of the decision makers. Can't this kind of facility be taken further? Using another approach, isn't management education the solution to the comprehension span problem?

Certainly the computer's ability to explore the effects of changing assumptions could be of great assistance to management. Just as the effect of different economic options open to government can be checked out on a computerized model of the total economy, so could all options open to a manager. There is much work in progress attempting to find a generally applicable way of modeling the flows of information, of goods, activities, or money in organizations. No doubt in time these models may become close enough to the reality to be more useful than the oversimplifications of the present. Whether they will ever be able to replicate the emotions, needs, and beliefs of the human beings that lie behind the equations in the models is another matter. The essence of being human lies in our ability to override our own predictions. This "essential humanness" may be the unbridgeable gap in the modeling approach to management.

So far, the attempt to educate for conceptual span has been another of those searches for the elusive Holy Grail. Techniques can be taught, information transferred, and skills acquired, by practice and coaching. But the ability to embrace complexity, or the *cathedral mentality* (to envision or start something whose completion you will not live to see), is less common. Some people maintain that such an ability must be inherited, or at least acquired, in those precious first years. Others argue that one can learn to think conceptually, that the study of history, economics, business case-studies, and even literature can bring out whatever latent abilities there are to see patterns in things and to look beyond the particular to the general. Yet there is little evidence for this. And if the ability can be acquired at a mature age, then assuredly it requires more time and attention than the four-week course that is the most that any practicing manager would feel justified in devoting to it.

We must conclude that at present, neither computers nor education offers a likely or a quick way out of the Apollonian impasse.

Does Education Help?

To most people, education means learning useful things, be they facts or techniques. In that sense, most further or higher education has an effective usefulness of about ten years maximum. After that, either the knowledge is outdated by advancing technology and new discoveries, or the individual has moved to a level or an occupation in which he no longer needs it. How many forty-year-olds are still using anything they learned in school or college?

But it may be that higher education creates or improves the ability to cope with complexity, to deal with issues rather than facts and the abstract as well as the particular. Watch what people talk about. Can they reason? Do they deal only with facts, turn opinion into fact, shun logical discussion? Is this related to their educational background?

In a 1968 study of the relative profitability of American subsidiaries in Britain, J. H. Dunning was able to demonstrate that American and British firms whose executives had degrees or equivalent formal qualifications earned considerably higher profits than those who did not.[9] It is noteworthy too that although this relationship is broadly the same for both the American and British firms in the sample, a much higher proportion of executives in American firms had university degrees or equivalent formal qualifications.

The cross-cultural comparison does not apply only to the United States. Fewer executives have degrees in Britain than in any other Western European country or Japan, as Handy showed twenty years later.[10]

Does this mean anything in terms of relative managerial ability, or is it only a reflection of different cultural fashions?

The second strand of resistance had to do with the essential "sin" of the Apollonian culture, which makes it an alienating place for the individual. The counter to this strand is not a denial but an acknowledgment that in any society and in any organization there must be a lot of boring jobs. Roles must take priority over individuals. For most people, work is something that has to be done in order that the rest of life may be enjoyed. There are, of course, those fortunate few whose work is their hobby. Wasn't happiness once defined as "being paid for your hobby"? For the rest, it obviously is important that work be made as painless as possible, that the physical conditions of work are congenial (but how can you make a foundry congenial?), and that the contractual side of employment is fair. And most important, the rewards of harder work, whether they be in money or increased leisure time, must be seen to be adequate. Here, it is argued, is the modern rub. The equation is not clear; more money is not linked closely enough to more work when clever negotiating or hijacking tactics can win the money without the work. Even when increased rewards do flow from increased productivity, penal personal taxation robs the individual of most of the fruit of his labor. If today the game of work is no longer worth the candle, the fault lies in the candle, not in the game.

There is, however, a fatal flaw creeping into this age-old argument. One man's rewards are too often now another man's grudge. Fred Hirsch, in an important book entitled *The Social Limits to Growth*, calls this dilemma the false promise of the affluent society.

It works like this: As long as you don't mind everyone else's having what you've got, you can offer the same carrot all round, and it will work as a universal incentive. So far so good. Plentiful food, better heating, more leisure—these are things that all people might want all others to have as well as themselves. But there are a whole lot of things we want that, by definition, all others cannot have because they depend on comparative advantage. Private education is one of them in Britain: Offer it to everyone, and it will cease to be desirable. Servants used to be another, but we all cannot be masters, for who then would serve? A house with an unspoiled view? If all had them, we would end up looking at one another in that view. Once we move from universal goods to comparative goods, we come up against the endless paradox: "When you've got what you want, you don't want what you've got, because everyone else has got it, too." The majority cannot enjoy a minority right.

When people are hungry, incentives work universally. When they work for comparative advantage, then increasing the incentives for some will only make others discontented. As they catch up, the effort from the first group will fall away. It is like walking up the down escalator. Apart from anything else, it is a built-in inflationary pressure.

"Let them go hungry, then." Indeed, a dose of massive deflation, unemployment, and siege economy conditions would soon bring back the universal incentive side of money. The counterargument to the second strand of resistance to Apollo would then be justified. But to use hunger as the lever to organizational efficiency is not politically acceptable today. We should be glad.

Does Money Matter?

Studies of both British and American organizations have consistently shown that a substantial pay rise (over 10 percent in net pay) does produce increased effort, energy, and enthusiasm—for an average period of six weeks. Thereafter, the new pay becomes the new baseline.

Questioned by Nancy Morse and Robert Weiss in the United States, 80 percent of 401 employed men said that they would continue working even if they did not need the money.[11]

In a study of British managers by Harry Hansen, the personal objective "to earn a substantial amount of money" ranked well below the other objectives:[12]

"Have freedom to carry out your own ideas, a chance for originality and initiative."
"Belong to a growing, successful organization."
"Work with associates whom you personally like."

The third strand concerned the changing values and norms of society as revealed in our educational methods and our child-rearing habits. The attention given to personal expression, to the development of one's own talents, to group activities, to influence through persuasion, and to a search for common purposes—Dionysian and Athenian attitudes—is antithetical to the impersonality, conformity, and obedience required in Apollonian systems. The counter to this strand might be to revert to more traditional ways of bringing up our young. In Britain, as in France, the Netherlands, the United States and parts of Germany, education was in the forefront of public attention following the student unrest of 1968. In all these countries, many argue for a return to former ways, and their arguments are based as much on the need to reestablish the traditional patterns of authority as on the efficiency of the learning methods. They maintain that the young, the less extroverted, the ordinary majority of working folk, need and appreciate structure and discipline in their lives. Too much, it is claimed, has been given and promised to the young. The pendulum must swing back, and the disappearance of the "youth bulge" in the population statistics of all countries will help push youth back in their place as a minority apprentice group in society.

To a degree, they must be correct in their predictions. In 1965, over half the population of the United States was under twenty-five. Now, in the mid-1990s, over half are over forty. Society will be middle aged; youth will be in a minority; and so middle-aged values of stability and security will prevail. There are even some worries that one day there may not be a large enough working population to fill the available jobs.

Nonetheless, there does seem to have been a radical shift in society's attitude toward the individual, a shift of which our educational philosophy is only a mirror, even if a slightly distorting one. If that is so, then organizations cannot ever again expect to rely on an obedient, complacent, dependent workforce. Democracy has worked its way through to the workplace, but Apollo prefers to ignore the democratic process. The clock cannot be turned back, even if its rate of change has slowed down, even if it is halted for a time. Our organizations will increasingly be populated by people who are Dionysians and Athenians at heart, with the occasional Zeus to flavor the mix. Necessity will make Apollonians out of many of them, at least on the surface. Many of them will not have the talent or abilities to sustain a Dionysian or Athenian job, inside or outside the organization. Hunger will breed conformity in some, but it will be a reluctant conformity, one that fertilizes negative power, absenteeism, and hijacks. And although there will be some who are true Apollonians—the tidy minded, those prepared to subordinate self to system—they will not be enough to staff the megabureaucracies pushed on us by the pressures for bigness and consistency.

The conclusion begins to seem inescapable. The three strands, or tendencies, that frustrate the Apollonian logic of the large organization will neither fade away nor be overcome in today's world. The visible result is expense—the expense of buying off hijacks, of staffing up for absenteeism, of compensating for the incapacity of the humans at the top: *slack*. For a time, in monopoly or quasimonopoly situations, when your competitors are in a similar state, the extra expense can be concealed by higher prices. In some few cases, a technological breakthrough or a giant step up the economies of scale will so lower the cost of production or service that the expense of the Apollonian system is absorbed—for a time. But there is no end to the possible costs of Apollo. In the end, the inflationary pressures of overpricing force themselves into the wider society. In competitive situations, the collapse comes sooner and is confined to the individual enterprise.

This, then, is the crossroads for the organization, particularly for the megabureaucracies of government and industry. Will they commit themselves to the ultimate victory of bigness and consistency, heads down as they go, believing that the resistances are little local difficulties? Or will they change course? Although the resulting decisions will be hugely important to the 90 percent who work in organizations, and therefore crucial decisions for society, the issue is not a political one or an ideological one, but a practical question of the design and management of organizations. It is not that the megabureaucracies are irresponsible corporations taking over from the state: The truth is that they may be too expensive because they have become, literally, unmanageable.

Today's dilemma was foreseen, of course. Keynes, an economist, perceived that his theories of economics were the economics of scarcity. Once scarcity had been eliminated, the central theories might lose their validity.

Keynes, the Post-Keynesian

In 1930, John Maynard Keynes looked forward in an essay to the "Economic Possibilities for our Grandchildren."[13] He prophesied that his grandchildren (who would be adults today) would discover that the "economic problem is not the permanent problem of the human race." He went on, "If the economic problem is solved, mankind will be deprived of its traditional purposes. Will this be a benefit? If one believes at all in the real values of life, the prospect at least opens up the possibility of benefit, yet I think with dread of the readjustments of the habits and instincts of the ordinary man, bred into him for countless generations, which he may be asked to discard within a few decades. . . .

The strenuous purposeful moneymakers may carry all of us along with them into the lap of economic abundance . . . but the rest of us will no longer be under any obligation to applaud and encourage them for we shall enquire more curiously than is safe today into the true character of this purposiveness . . . for purposiveness means that we are more concerned with the remote future results of our actions than with their own quality or their immediate effects on our environments."

Gurth Higgin argued convincingly that since the Middle Ages, the whole thrust of society has been toward the elimination of scarcity. Now that this is potentially a solved problem in the industrialized world, society is searching for a new thrust, and old values and systems and codes of behavior come into question. When scarcity was the enemy, then much could be tolerated in the name of efficiency. The organization was the instrument of society and men, machines and money the instruments of the organization. When scarcity is no longer a common enemy, except in time of war or natural disaster, the costs of efficiency begin to seem high.

6

Reactions

The Apollonian dilemma is not new. We all have been aware for a long time that the disciplines that efficiency seems to require are not always palatable to free people. Marx may or may not have exaggerated when he compared industrial organizations with the institutions of slavery, but he has always had many sympathizers, many of them vehement. For a long time, society could afford to ignore the dilemma. The results of efficiency in terms of more to eat and spend, of years lived and comforts enjoyed, were obviously worth the costs of organizational discipline for society as a whole. Of course, the benefits were not always as well distributed as they might have been, but political pressures could be relied on to put that right in the end. But that cost–benefit equation is no longer so obvious today, when there appear to be diminishing returns to the individual from increased efficiency. The game is no longer worth so much candle, and the dilemma of Apollo has become more urgent as a result.

We can detect in society various attitudes and responses to the dilemma. None of them seems to me to be adequate. Some of them even compound the problem. Yet we need to examine them, if only to dismiss them, because they make up the conventional wisdom in this field. Let me describe them briefly.

One attitude relies on a staunch belief in the inexorable logic

Never Will So Many Owe So Much to So Few

of efficiency. That is, more growth will once again make the game worthwhile. In effect, if the theory of cultural propriety succeeded in eliminating slack, we would once again be swallowed up in the common objective of material growth. Others, however, would accept that we need impossible rates of growth to keep us all profitably employed. To them the solution lies in creating a sort of industrial meritocracy that would create wealth so that the rest of us might live. The preconditions of their view are that the meritocracy be properly rewarded and that the rest of us be educated for leisure, or life without employment. Both these views have, of course, a lot of popular support, but I argue that they do not present us with a long-term solution to the need to blend efficiency with individualism for the whole of society.

Then there are those who see organizations as inevitable and as inevitably diminishing to the individual. The pressures of efficiency need, as they see it, to be balanced by pressures for individual rights in organizations. Democracy must apply to work as well to the wider society. Many of these democratic enthusiasts would have their cake as well as eat it, by maintaining that more democracy would bring more efficiency. Others are more realistic, recognizing that democracy has never been known for efficiency but maintaining that it is a necessary precondition of human relationships in a civilized society (cost what it may, they might add). There is, finally, a lower-key variant of full democracy that argues for practical participation and organization on a human scale. I would have more sympathy with this last approach if I felt that it was genuinely concerned with the dilemma of human dignity at work and not merely tinkering with the distorting effects of excessive alienation.

The arguments among the exponents of these different viewpoints are often violent. The diverging perspectives of the "industrial meritocracy" view and that of the "full democracy" stance do in fact color the whole of our political debate. To call it a debate is to dignify it, for usually the advocates of each view cannot understand or even hear what the others are saying. Society sometimes seems to be tearing itself apart over this Apollonian dilemma. The debates go on in private, too, as the following example demonstrates.

When Auntie Came to Dinner

My aunt by marriage is a splendid character, but from a bygone age. Her father never worked, nor his father before him, nor, of course, had she ever earned a penny in her life. Their capital worked for them, and they managed their capital. Work was done by workers. She sees all governments today as insanely prejudiced against capital, all workers as inherently greedy and lazy, and most managements as incompetent. No wonder that the world is in a mess and she getting poorer every day.

Tony is a friend from work. His father was a postman. He started life as a draftsman in a large engineering firm. He grew up believing that inherited capital was socially wrong. He had never met any man who did not or had not worked for his living.

My aunt and Tony met by chance at my house over a meal. It started quietly, politely. Then she inquired what he did. It transpired that he had recently joined his staff union. Auntie had never met a union member.

"Good heavens, how could you?" she said.

"It makes very good sense," said Tony, "to protect your rights."

"What rights? What poppycock is this? If people like you spent more time at their work and less looking after their own interests, this country wouldn't be in its present mess."

"Don't you," said Tony, "spend your time looking after your rights?"

"Of course," she said, "but then, I've got rights. I provide the money that makes it possible for people like you to live."

"I provide the labor that keeps your money alive, although why I should work to preserve the capital of rich people whom I've never met is something that puzzles me."

"You talk like a Communist, young man, although you dress quite respectably. Do you know what you're saying?"

"You don't have to be a Communist to question the legitimacy of inherited wealth."

My aunt turned to me.

"You see why I'm worried about this country?" she said.

Each regarded the other as an example of an un-
natural species. Given their opposed "core beliefs," no
proper argument or dialogue was possible, only an exchange of slogans or abuse. It is a score that is replicated
at negotiating tables as well as dinner tables.

Let us now examine these unavailing responses in a little more
detail.

The First Response

The first line of response to the Apollonian crisis sees organizations as the instruments of an efficient and effective society. We
could not get richer without them, nor could we be looked after
when ill, be educated, protected, or serviced in the ways we are
accustomed to. It is therefore a citizen's duty and responsibility
to put up with the disciplines of work in return for the benefits
of belonging to society.

Responsibility is the key word in this approach. It is irresponsible to negotiate high pay increases when these would hamper the
efficiency of the organization or force it to put others out of
work. People need to be educated to understand where their
responsibilities and their best long-term interests lie, and they
need to be disciplined by an efficient labor market that keeps
wages and salaries competitive and allows organizations to get
rid of inefficient workers.

Apollonian organizations, in this view of things, may not be
fun palaces for everyone, but they are justified in the end by the
greater benefit they produce for all. The end, in this case, justifies the means. One has only to look at places like Hong Kong, in
its heyday of the late 1970s and early 1980s. Work was work, but
it was abundantly justified by the results.

The Anti-Industrial English

Martin Wiener, who teaches history at Rice University in
Texas, produced a devastating analysis of the British atti-
tudes toward industry.[1] He argued that almost as soon as
Britain began to industrialize it surrounded the social

change in a cultural cocoon that muffled industrialism and prevented its full effects.

The idea of an English gentleman, and a gentlemanly attitude of disdain for trade, played a big part. Successful industrialists wanted their sons to become educated gentlemen and country squires, not to succeed them at "the works." The English dream was of the countryside, stability, and an "epoch of rest," as William Morris called it.

Education preferred "science" to "engineering" and the arts to both. Agriculture and the ownership of land were preferable to business and the ownership of machinery. The professions, including the armed forces, were socially superior to industry.

In the United States, the culture was different. Business was respectable, and therefore it has thrived.

When advocacy fails and the wolf cries of newspapers are ignored, this response falls back on the discipline of the economic pendulum to return people to their (Apollonian) senses.

It may be, they will say, that in the short term, one must envisage the progressive overpricing of our outputs because of the cost of large Apollonian systems operating amid current popular values. This overpricing can be sustained artificially for a time by a lower exchange rate, by large external borrowings, by import controls, and by selective earnings. In the end, however, we shall run out of mechanisms, and the threat of scarcity will no longer be a threat but a perceived reality. Efficiency in the face of this common enemy will then once again be seen to be worth its costs, in terms of lost individualism. We shall no longer take things for granted but will start to instill the virtues of discipline, conformity, and obedience in our children. In return, the organization will, on its part, revert to the obligations it used to have, to provide work and careers for life. Look at the Japanese. For a time after the war, they embraced American ideas of individualism and American practices of management in their organizations. After a period of vicious inflation and political immobility, they returned to an organizational contract that exchanged protection for commitment, supported it with more traditional education systems, and arranged for their own form of participation at work, a unique concept of "groupism." It could happen here in the West, but only if we grow hungry enough. Maybe, the travelers on this road would argue, things will have to get worse in every country before they can get better. The Apollonians who contend this believe that it is the country, the people who make up the country, who are out of step, not them. Time, with some pain, will bring them back to their rightful culture.

Alas, the pendulum swings both ways. Maybe hunger would make us Apollonian once more, but as soon as efficiency re-turned us to abundance, wouldn't the problems recur? Isn't this a route to a generational stop–go cycle of a more traumatic kind than the minor economic ones of the past twenty years? There are signs already of a return to individualism in Japanese society.

The second danger is that as they seek to delay the sweep of the pendulum and the ultimately inevitable hunger, governments may make changes that will be more fundamental and more long lasting than any mere import controls or rationing procedures. It is doubtful, for instance, whether any stock exchange would be willing or able to provide the desired quantities of new investment in the desired areas under the conditions of overpricing in the first part of this scenario. Government would then be forced to step in, first as the banker of last resort and ultimately as the prime source of new investment. This is the economic road to totalitarian rule, with the increased bureaucracy that would inevitably accompany it—compounding Apollo everywhere. Governments, furthermore, in an attempt to hold back the damaging costs of organizational hijacks, would be forced to collude with any that could guarantee labor peace, even at the long-term cost of overhiring. This temporary bypassing of the democratic process may leave permanent damage by downgrading the whole notion of electoral democracy. Thus, by a process of successive expedients, without conscious aim, a nation can be forced into government by edict. And once the economic and political mechanisms of a more responsive democracy have been allowed to wither, they may not bloom again for a long time. Democracy might be the price one has to pay for underwriting Apollo as the principal god of the organized society. Is our hunger great enough?

The Second Response

The second response to the Apollonian crisis would make organizational work not a duty but a privilege. Employment in a large organization would be for the minority and not the majority. The organizations, slimmed down and properly automated, would need to employ only two classes of people—core professionals and flexible labor—both kept to a minimum and well paid. The rest could be contracted out. If it were a privilege to belong to the organization, its drills and disciplines would be readily accepted and adhered to. Apollo would be honored.

The organization would employ only those that it absolutely had to—the managers, experts, and skilled technicians who together possessed the organizational knowledge that made the organization special and unique (the core professionals), and a labor force, mostly semiskilled, to carry out any tasks that could not be automated. Everything else either could be contracted out to people or groups who provided similar services to other organizations, or could be automated if more money and technology were invested.

Organizations, in other words, would be sought-after places because of the security they offered or the money, or sometimes both. Money would compensate for antisocial hours, one-sided contracts, or uncongenial work. Key people would be promised careers and a variety of perks. The extra cost involved would be paid for by increased productivity, which is another way of saying that there would be fewer people in the organizations or around them. Employment would be rationed and therefore privileged. In return for this privilege, the disciplines of Apollo could be enforced. The dilemma of Apollo would thereby be, in effect, bought out.

High Pay for Low Work?

There was an interesting exchange of letters in a British newspaper not so long ago.

The head of one of Britain's newer universities wrote to complain about the low numbers and poor quality of the students applying to enter his university.

"It is, perhaps," he said, "hardly to be wondered at.

After all, the salary which they are likely to receive on leaving will probably be less than that earned by a new or unskilled recruit to an assembly line in a car plant."

Four days later, the paper printed a reply from a shop steward in a car plant.

"No doubt," said the letter, "the vice chancellor has never worked on an assembly line. If he had, he would not wish his graduates to find their employment there. As a result of their education at his university, they will find jobs in pleasant surroundings, with an opportunity to use their talents and influence events around them. Is it not fair that my lads, deprived of these things, should get more money by way of compensation?"

A recent calculation showed that already, today, in Britain if one man decided to become an academic and eventually a professor and his brother stayed at his job as an engineering fitter, the professor would be fifty-four before his accumulated lifetime earnings would overtake those of his brother.

Fair or unfair?

It would be the Japanese way, for work in Japan is not all that it is reported to be—at least not for everybody. Lifetime employment is not for all workers but only for those who work for the big corporations, perhaps 30 percent of the labor force at most, for Japan's corporations contract out as much of their work and their labor requirements as possible. For the minority that is permanently employed, life is secure and predictable, but for the rest it can often be precarious and impoverished.

Working in Japan

The big Japanese corporation floats on a raft of subcontractors. A typical car maker, like Toyota, would have 36,000 subcontractors, of whom 35,000 would be small businesses with less than 100 employees.

Lifetime employment applies only to the 30 percent of workers who are employed by the large corporations, and this "lifetime" employment ends at age fifty-five. The individual is then, one hopes, but not necessarily, hired by one of the subcontracting firms, to which his organizational knowledge can be important.

Self-employment is big stuff in Japan. There are, according to OECD statistics, 19 percent self-employed in Japan, compared with 12 percent in the United States, and there is a further 10 percent categorized as "unpaid domestic workers." Self-employed people cannot, by logic or by law, be unemployed, although they may be poor. Part of Japan's concealed unemployment may be in this category, as well as in the "seat warmers" of the large corporations.

Perhaps it is not so surprising that the inhabitants of Japan's Apollonian temples are so happy to conform with their ways. Maybe in Britain the feeling of privilege would outweigh the irritations of the Apollonian disciplines.

It is a possible future, but one fraught with social peril. It was a talented young woman who said to me, "There will always be jobs for people like me, and I think that we should be prepared to pay extra taxes so that the rest can live in reasonable comfort and even go to Europe for vacation." She meant well, but she was describing a society split in two, one in which the "working class," by an ironic twitch of fate, had become the privileged one and the "leisure class" was now the deprived one. The last time that happened was in Imperial Rome, and the precedent is not encouraging. Hi-tech alternatives to the bread and circuses of those days may be no more satisfying than the originals were. Dependency, it seems, pleases neither the giver, particularly if the giving is compulsory, nor the getter.

Secure careers and high wages for a few may help make Apollo both smaller and more bearable, but it is debatable whether the price is worth it or whether it is a sustainable solution when there are likely to be so many left on the outside. Slimmed-down professional organizations are, we shall argue, part of a viable future, but they will be ones in which Apollo is really the servant and not the master. Turning Apollonian organizations into a meritocracy may be tempting to those inside, but it is a recipe—in Europe, at least—for a divided and divisive society.

In any case, there is some evidence that the privilege is not enough to convert Athenians and Dionysians into willing Apollonians. It could be that the employment organization, left in its

Apollonian state, might end up as the refuse heap of the organized society, left with all those who could not cope outside.

Pros and Antis in American Companies

An American study investigated procompany and anticompany attitudes among organization employees.[2] The procompany people turned out to be competent, self-assured, and independent. The "antis" despised and condemned the firm they worked for, although not many ever left it. The disgruntled anticompany workers were found to be personality types who needed a lot of sympathy and support from others. When support did not come from the company, they turned to unions and professional associations.

Ironically, it seems to be the Dionysians, or at least the Athenians, who are at ease, not the Apollonians. Who would lose out in the meritocratic organization? Would they let it happen?

The Third Response

The third response to the Apollonian dilemma goes beyond the ideas of duty or privilege to democracy. The organization, it agrees, is central to an effective society. It should, therefore, be a better reflection of that society, because it is in fact one of the principal *communities* of that society.

Already we can see how the state uses the work organization as its favored administrative community. Whenever possible, taxes are collected through the work organization, not the local authority. Legislation on incomes, on equality of opportunity and treatment, and on the treatment of the disabled or the underprivileged is enforced through the work organization, because this is where most of the people spend most of their time.

If, then, the organization is the new community, it is appropriate that the rights of the individual be extended to that community. What does this mean? What are these rights? The normal citizenship rights in a democracy include the following:

The right of tenure (or protection against eviction without due process of law), in organizational terms, the right to a job.

The right of appeal, if decisions affecting an individual are disputed.

The right to information, if that information has any impact on oneself.

The right of free speech, as long as neither treason nor libel is involved.

The right to elect one's own rulers and occasionally the right, in referenda, to tell them what to do.

Increasingly, it is pointed out, we see these rights being brought into the organization. In the smaller organizations, they exist informally. It is because they do not exist widely enough in enough places that they are not imposed by legislation. It is a recognition of what the European Union calls "the democratic imperative."

These rights are not, this third approach might claim, anything to be unduly alarmed about. They are merely a recognition, in legal terms, of something that has been readily accepted by many managers for a long time: that an organization is as responsible to those who provide its labor as it is to those who provide its capital, its shareholders. Indeed, since more and more of this capital comes from retained earnings (i.e., from labor), the responsibility to the workforce must far outweigh that to the original owners.

Now that scarcity is potentially a solved problem, we are really talking about comparative degrees of abundance. The organization, therefore, is no longer an instrument of society; it is much more than that; it is part of the main body of society, a fact that must be reflected in the way it is run. A community is a collection of individuals who must be allowed their individual rights. Life, liberty, and the pursuit of justice are not valid only in the home or the sports arena—they must be carried into the factory, the office, the hospital, the field, everywhere that people work.

There are even, it is argued, long-term economic grounds for this legislation for individual rights. The large organizations are essential to maintain our societies in that precarious state of modern abundance that we have now achieved. The collapse of these organizations would return us to that scarcity from which we have only recently managed to haul ourselves. Yet these organizations are now so powerful, so dominating, and often so alienating that people will not work in them and will not join them, or contemplate joining them, unless they can be assured of some countervailing power, of the protection of the law and the state. There are already enough incentives for those who rule these corporations to be efficient. Let there be some pressures for individualism.

We would be foolish, however, or at least naive, to think that a better charter of individual rights would be enough to redeem Apollo. Necessary though it may be, sufficient it will seldom prove to be. Indeed, the first effect would be to compound Apollo, creating yet more bureaucratic hurdles, more "no entry" signs in front of possible decision paths, more tribunals, more arbitrations, and more lawyers' tangles. It is right that an individual at work should have the same protections and the same opportunities as a citizen at large has, but although it may mean that the worst abuses of organizations are prevented, it won't make them any less complex or any more fun or free for the individual. It may be an understandable, even inevitable, response to the growing crisis of Apollo, but it will not solve that crisis. We must go beyond a bill of rights.

There are some who think differently. Apollo made secure will, they believe, be Apollo welcomed. They see the organization as existing for those who work in it. Markets must be expanded and profits increased to provide more work and better guarantees of what work there already is. They have some evidence to prove them right, but they are few, and although they are big enough to influence their destinies and to ride out the storms, they may yet prove to be running against a tide of values.

Job Tenure Pays Off

In December 1982, the workforce at Delta Airlines gave their employer a gift of a Boeing 767. It was, in a way, a thank you to the firm for its policy of no layoffs. Delta had not made anyone redundant since 1956. Nor, at that time, had IBM. Others, such as Hewlett-Packard, Avon Products, and Bank of America sought to follow their example, in the belief that such a policy built loyalty, confidence, and trust in management; less resistance to technical change; lower staff turnover; and better employee relations. They put the trust back into Apollo, Japanese style.

Such policies, however, bring problems, as these companies discovered. Firms must hold back on government business, which comes in chunks that may not always be renewed; they cannot be too aggressive in looking for more market share, in case it cannot be maintained; they must reduce pressure on earnings in lean times by keeping their debt low and their dividends small; and they must be prepared to build up stock rather than lay off workers.

Not surprisingly, therefore, Foulkes and Whitman found only thirty American companies that followed such policies, and they were all big ones in relatively stable industries.[3]

Call it what you will—industrial democracy, participation, the protection of individual rights—this road to the future must be a Dionysian charter. Even its advocates might admit that the enforcement of these rights, however necessary, would hamper short-term efficiency. It might do more than that. It might tilt the balance of power so much toward the individual that the management of large organizations would become impossible. The emerging bill of rights would be seen as a license to use negative power if there were not the opposing draw of commitment, dedication, and service. Yet to create these conditions in a large formal organization is perhaps to ask too much of any leaders. Warren Bennis, then head of one of those huge American multiversities, in Cincinnati, wrote about the "politics of multiple advocacies" in which pressure groups spring up (he had to contend with more than five hundred in his university alone) to "represent people who are fed up with being ignored, neglected, excluded, denied, subordinated. No longer, however, do they march on cities, or bureaus, or on organizations. . . . Now they file suit. The law has suddenly emerged as the court of first resort." He asks, "Where have all the leaders gone? They are all scared," he concludes, "and who can blame them?"

This formal enfranchisement of the individual, this organizational bill of rights, is, when one thinks of it, an Apollonian response to individualism. "Codify it, formalize it, institute procedures" is the Apollonian way. Such a response may do no more than acknowledge the legitimacy of individualism in organizations. It will not be enough to contain it. "Industrial democracy," which turns out to be a modest attempt to introduce formal representative democracy into the central government of organizations, may well turn out to be as full of false promise as representative democracy traditionally has been in the wider society. It may, as it spreads, signal the complaint rather than cure it—like colored ointments on a boil—leaving the true disease to fester underneath. In 1977 in Britain, the Bullock Committee on Industrial Democracy published its proposals for the formal representation at the board level of the employees of large industrial organizations. The general reaction was that the problem (of industrial democracy) was much bigger than the proposed solutions (of formal representation) and that the detailed proposals might actually cause more problems than they solved.

There is, however, a more pragmatic variant of the democratic imperative. Organizations are communities, true, say such people. But the only communities that mean anything are small ones, communities that have to do with individuals and their personal hopes, fears, activities, and friendships. In the organization, that community must be the immediate work group, the ten or a dozen or twenty people that converge on a particular task. If participation is to mean anything, it is at this level where it will matter. If individualism must be expressed, then it is here that it would be most appropriate.

Volvo led the way in redesigning an engine shop that would allow the group to organize its own work. Why did Volvo do this? Because the workforce that it had traditionally used on the traditional assembly line had to return home. They were Finns, working as aliens in Sweden for the higher wages of that country: hungry or greedy people tolerating Apollonian restrictions for the money. Swedes, however, were less hungry or more greedy (depending on how you look at it), and they were less prepared to accept the alienating procedures for that sort of money. So the work was redesigned.

There are now innumerable examples of firms' handing over more responsibility to work groups, breaking down assembly lines, and lengthening job cycles so that each worker does more than one operation. The results nearly always include a lower rate of absenteeism and sickness, better overall morale, and often better quality. In one typewriter plant in West Berlin, for instance, typewriters used to be assembled on two lines, each nearly five hundred feet long; each employee had a repetitive job cycle of six minutes each. It was boring work, with social contact limited to the people on either side. The line was then replaced with six shorter lines, each worked by a team. The teams developed a system of "mutual obligations" which allowed people to take time off for sickness or refreshment. They increased the job cycle to twenty-four minutes and were allowed to choose their own teams. Morale, turnover, and quality all improved.

Often, however, these ideas are sparked by the general thesis that smallness is not only beautiful but also economically efficient. The difficulties in organizing larger complex organizations (referred to in an earlier chapter as the *first strand of resistance*) can be very expensive. H. G. Van Beck, of the Phillips plant at Eindhoven, Holland, described how he split up the 104-man assembly line into five groups with buffer stocks between each group. As a result, the waiting time caused by lack of material fell by 45 percent, and the workers experienced the higher morale and lower absenteeism that could have been expected.

Small is Efficient

Small firms have fewer industrial disputes. In the bad days of the 1970s in Britain, firms with more than 1,000 employees lost 2,000 days per year per 1,000 workers, compared with 15 days per year for firms with fewer than 25 workers.

Evidence collected in Wales and England on farm performance suggests that very small farms are inefficient but that once the three-man unit has been reached, further improvements in performance are small or nonexistent.[4]

Most firms reach their maximum efficient size when they control 10 percent of the market. After that, for all but a handful of companies, the ratio between profit and size does not change, however large the company grows, although there is less danger of fluctuations in profit in a large operation.

When Serck Audio Valves pioneered the idea of manufacturing "cells" in its factory (these were, effectively, self-contained manufacturing units, or "villages"), its sales went up 32 percent; its stocks (the slack in an Apollo system) went down 44 percent; and the the output per employee increased 60 percent in the first five years.[5]

There is now a whole movement, grandiosely entitled the "quality of working life," that seeks to promote, through research and the dissemination of results, this approach to the design of the more boring jobs. No one can deny that it is sensible. We know quite a lot about boring, repetitive work, or the microdivision of labor, as it has been called.

• The microdivision of labor induces fatigue, boredom, distractions, accidents, and anxieties. The indirect costs of these things are reflected in spoilage, absenteeism, and high staff turnover.

• The true costs of monotony are in the very high wages for low skill level, high rates of strikes, and waste.

• People, unlike machines, work more efficiently at a variable than at a constant rate.

• Moderately complicated tasks resist interruptions and generate psychological impulses toward their own completion.

• Excessive specialization reduces the opportunity for social contact or teamwork. Long periods of unrelieved isolation are hard for people to tolerate.

Isn't it then just good sense to put some variety into the job? Are we really dealing with people's need to express themselves at work? Many of the studies of job redesign show a gradual return to the old norms of morale and absenteeism once the changes have become adopted as the new routine. A twenty-four-minute job cycle is much more interesting than a three-minute one, but given the tolerance to which it has to be done, the eventual anonymity of the product, and the remoteness of the end use, is it really such a big deal? One study discovered that the workers in small towns and factories responded well to the redesign of their work but that the workers in large cities showed no response or reaction at all. The research called them "anomic," rendered insensitive by large-city life. Perhaps they were not duped: It would take more than an enlarged job cycle to get them to put their identities into their work.

A Mirage of Dionysus?

The autonomous work group is the nearest that most large, formal organizations have come to recognizing the pressures of individualism.

The idea of an autonomous group is that a work group becomes responsible for organizing its own system of working, job rotation, quality inspection, leave roster, and so on. The foreman becomes a liaison man with other groups, a provider of information, but not a boss. The following example from Denmark shows how it works, but there are now many examples from all the industrialized countries.

In a factory producing measuring instruments, the assembly section was reorganized into autonomous groups. All groups are made up of skilled and unskilled workers (both men and women). The groups themselves divide the work. The groups cooperate intensively with the quality control section, and now other groups and the control section discuss each batch together. The workers state that they find it more meaningful to work with a whole apparatus rather than a part, because no one has any idea what the parts are. Several find that they are more concerned with one another in the work group and that they learn more. Productivity rose 25 percent.

No one can quarrel with this way of organizing work, but is it enough? The workers' final comments speak for themselves:

"The firm is a profit-oriented enterprise, and we come here only for the sake of the money, but that does not keep us from making our daily work as pleasant as possible."

Autonomous groups offer only a mirage of Dionysus. The real thing will have to be much more significant.

It is possible that organizations adopting this approach can hold Dionysus at bay for a time. But today's change will quickly become tomorrow's routine. The Dionysian cult does not pertain to monotony at work but to the whole relationship of organization, individual, and society. This approach does nothing to change that relationship, and so it is not, therefore, likely to be the true road to the future.

Growth, of course, we need, and the efficiency that produces it. But at what price, and paid for by whom? Do any of the views we discussed contain the true solution? Confirmed Apollonians will stick to their guns, modifying their ways, perhaps, to accommodate the "autonomy" of the last approach as long as it can be demonstrated to improve efficiency. The meritocrats will continue to work toward their ideal of the slimmed-down organization, properly rewarded. The more modest and humble will settle for a bill of rights: some, behind it, will play their game of economic brinkmanship with the managers and directors; others will settle for a quiet life, keeping their individualism for the garden.

In modern industrialized societies, we can see progress in all three approaches. None of them leads, on its own, to a future that we can want. A three-way split is painful as well as unproductive. If these ways will not work, what might? That is the theme of the next chapter.

7

The Gods
in New Order

We argued in the last two chapters that the *organizational* imperatives (for increased size and greater consistency) in our present
society are locked into an inevitable battle with the *individual*
imperatives (for greater opportunity for personal expression
and choice). It is a conflict that will not disappear. Nor, in my
view, is it a conflict that Apollo can win. If our organizations are
to survive, they must adapt their managerial philosophy to one
better suited to the needs, aspirations, and attitudes of individuals. In the new mix of the gods that will result, Apollo will be less
dominant and less inhuman. This will mean, however, a massive
change in the structure of organizations and their work.

We might describe the kind of change that is needed as a
switch from the employment organization to something more
like a combination of a professional partnership, a contractual
organization, and a federal state. Treating people as individuals
rather than human resources requires a culture and structure
more like that of a professional organization, in which each individual is qualified and certified, there are few levels of authority,
and the place is run by consent rather than decree. Professionals,
however, have tenure and cannot easily be laid off; nor will they
readily do the more mundane and boring jobs. To keep their
flexibility, therefore, organizations will need to combine a profes-

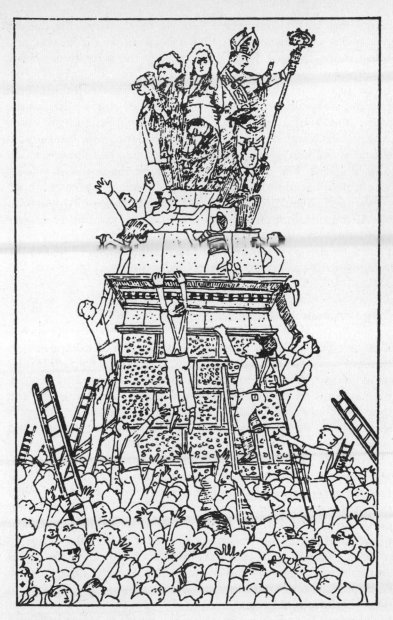

The New Professionals

sional core with a contractual element, on the basis that there is no need to employ people to do what others can do for you, and often more cheaply. Finally, to prevent the individual's being swamped by the size of the operation (and the Apollonian structures that come with size), organizations must keep their separate bits as small and as autonomous as they can, without at the same time losing all the advantages of bigness. Federalism, which is at its best a way of combining independence with interdependence, should increasingly become a model to be followed. Good organizations, like our best cities, will be made up of villages where people can be individuals and yet part of a greater whole.

We need to look, therefore, at the implications of the professional organization and the contractual organization to understand the ways in which the theory of cultural propriety is effected, or the gods rebalanced, which will entail a return to the village and the adoption of federalist notions.

The Professional Organization

The best way of looking at the pressures of individualism is to think of work as becoming increasingly professionalized. It is an ironic consequence of the specialization so beloved by Apollonian systems that everyone is now a specialist of some sort and that most jobs are skilled jobs, or are so termed. And every specialist, as we know, looks for the personal prerogatives and advantages of specialization, that is, professionalism.

Professionalism brings with it some advantages and some consequences. The advantages include a protected entry to the profession, agreed fee scales, and effective "tenure." Moved down a slot in the social scale, these become the closed shop, differentials, and guaranteed job security—all items in the managerial news these days. Only the managers seem to be left as unorganized professionals, as they have recently begun to realize. This emphasis on the terms and conditions of work is normal, even when scarcity and bread for one's family is no longer the critical issue, because to a professional his work is the major source of his identity. If one ceases to describe oneself in terms of where one lives or who one's father was, but in terms of one's trade, skill, or occupation, then the nature and style of that occupation will have great symbolic and real importance. Work is no longer a means of paying for the groceries; it is central to one's personal identity.

The case is similar for earnings. A professional, like a craftsman, is paid for his skill, not for his length of service or his loyalty. Differentials are important, for symbolic as well as economic reasons. The professional worker is concerned with using his skill to his maximum advantage, for his commitment is his profession before his organization, and we should not expect it to be otherwise. Professionals, therefore, will be mobile, with a reference group that extends across organizations. They will move, and be able to move, when they want to. Organizations must handle their good professionals gently, or they will disappear. The good professionals have effective tenure and may be expected to exploit this.

And professionalism means freedom, the freedom to express oneself and to be true to oneself (the Dionysian virtues). A professional puts his or her mark on the job: His is not an anonymous act, even though it conforms to a set of standards common to the profession. Freedom also implies that one is owned by no one and by no organization, even though one may lend it one's skills. This freedom of the personal-service professions is greatly sought after today. It is the personal-service professions of law and medicine whose schools have the highest application rates, not the impersonalized professions of the civil engineer or the industrial chemist, whose talents, on the other hand, may be in even greater demand. It is this freedom of the personal-service professions that the new specialists envy and would claim for their own.

Professionalism, of course, carries responsibilities, but they are responsibilities to the practice of one's trade, craft, or skill, not to an organization. Professions are likely, as a consequence, to be jealous of their traditional territories, to resist new developments not initiated by them, and to be generally conservative in many of their attitudes. Demarcation disputes are found in medicine and law, as well as in engineering, even if they go by other names. Today, in Britain, the legal profession is fighting to continue its monopoly in property transfers.

To be a recognized professional today, at any level of society, is to substitute the protection and the status of a trade for that of an organization. Work has become professionalized, and all people want to be treated as Dionysians or Athenians, whatever bit of the organization they work in or whatever the cultural demands of their work.

This spread of professionalism colors all the cults. Even the true believer in order, predictability, and system—the Apollonian—will be influenced by the wish to be treated as a recognized expert in the tradition of Athena, if not of Dionysus. It is this spread of professionalism that in the medium term will force us to change our ways of managing, for professionalism has added teeth to the forces resisting Apollo listed in Chapter 5. We may have been able to get away with lip service to cries for more individualism. But now we shall have to do more in the face of organized professionalism. Our starting models for the new ways of managing must be among the existing professional organizations.

"Universities," I said, "are the prototypes of the organizations of tomorrow."

"If that be so," said a professor standing near, "then God help us all."

Behind my remark was the suggestion that universities, rather like professional partnerships, mountain-climbing teams, and theatrical groups or orchestras, must be managed to be effective but must be managed by consent.

What is meant by an *organization of consent?* In these organizations, the "psychological contract" between individual and organization is implicit and has a particular slant. In traditional, more Apollonian organizations, the contract runs something like this:

> The individual is here because he has a particular talent or skill or aptitude or just a pair of hands; he is lending this resource to the organization in return for some mixture of money, facilities, excitement, or companionship, and he cedes to the organization the right to deploy this resource, himself, as it sees fit, within reasonable limits, often formally defined and negotiated.

If the organization violates this implicit contract—if, for instance, it offers more excitement or job satisfaction when all the individual wants is money, then it will run into difficulties.

In the organization of consent, the contract goes beyond this. For one thing, it has a very individual slant. A person sees himself as a valuable *person,* whom the organization should cherish, not just resource to deploy. He is very much an individual, with a personality, individual desires, and rights that the organization must respect. The contract also includes some deep beliefs about the way people should relate to one another. Hierarchy is bad. Argument is good. All men and women are on an equal footing.

We are talking, it is clear, about Athenian and Dionysian attitudes.

The manager in an organization of consent is meant to manage, to make decisions, set up information systems, to plan, and to organize. Each person believes that he has his own proper and valuable role to play, and nobody wants to do anyone else's work for him. But the important decisions—the right to institute procedures, to start things, to stop things, or to change major things—must be exposed to possible disagreement before being implemented. Although the people may not want to be involved, they do want to be consulted. They want to be unfettered but not unnoticed. The minority report may never be implemented, but it must be listened to.

Management by Consent

Once I had to manage one part of an organization by consent. I was trying to discuss why my instructions had not been carried out by a colleague whom I thought of as my subordinate.

"You cannot tell me to do something," he explained gently, "you can only ask me."

"On the other hand," he went on, rubbing salt into the wound, "I don't ask you if I'm going to do something, I tell you."

Similarly, a friend, moving into an organization of consent from a traditional hierarchical business, was dismayed to find that his circular memoranda and his published requirements of his associates produced absolutely no result at all, not even rebellion. Just silence. "Would you believe it?" he said, "I've had to go along and make an individual personal contact with each of them."

He got into further difficulties when he assumed that since his associates rejected his right to decide, they wanted to make all decisions themselves. Not so. "That's your job," they said. "We have other and better things to do than help you make your decisions. But we need to be consulted about those decisions before they go into effect."

It was not authority in itself that they were objecting to, but his assumption of that authority before it had been given to him. The distinction is tricky—but important.

Professional organizations are flat organizations; most have only four steps to the top layer of status, and anyone with talent and application would expect to be a full partner, professor, or board member by the age of forty. That results in a long list of names at the top. This list, however, is not the top line of the organization chart, for no one could run anything that way. Rather, the list is a recognition of professional status, but the work is organized into groups, teams, sections, or faculties—Athenian structures for Dionysians.

The Contractual Organization

Professionals are expensive and permanent, or to be more precise, if they are employed, they must be treated as if they were permanent. Few organizations therefore use their own professionals for things that other people can do equally well. They keep their professionals for the core tasks of the organization, including management. The remaining work they contract out to outside sources (called, in the jargon, *outsourcing*) or to various categories of temporary help. To be viable economically, the professional organization must be accompanied by the contractual organization.

The contractual organization works on the basis of paying *fees* rather than *wages*. Fees are paid for work done, whereas wages are paid for time spent. The fee payer is concerned whether the work performed or delivered is up to standard, on time, and in the right quantity. It is not his concern to motivate, control, or organize the time of his workers; to see their conditions of work or pension requirements. He does not have to house them, feed them, or counsel them while they work, but he also has less control over them.

There have always been organizations of contract. Independent professionals have always charged fees, and so have craftsmen, artists, and artisans. Publishers do not employ their authors or, indeed, their printers. Instead, they work entirely on the basis of contracts and fees, their role being that of the fixer in the middle. Architects, although responsible for the design and the construction of a building, do not employ all the talents necessary to do that—it would never occur to them that it was necessary or desirable to own and run a building firm. Advertising agencies do not employ the people who actually make the advertisements.

It used to be felt, in the days of the grand Apollonian organizations, that to control anything, you had to own it and employ all the people in it. That way you could make things happen your way. But this became expensive when the cleaners, caterers, drivers, and maintenance people all had to be offered the same terms and conditions, and even the same sort of career expectations, as the essential professionals. Increasingly, organizations started hiring outsiders to clean buildings, cook food, arrange travel, and drive vehicles. There was less direct control but also less cost. Almost all organizations today have a contractual fringe, called *outsourcing, privatization* (if in the public sector), or *subcontracting*. Contracting takes other and grander forms. One can subcontract the manufacture, as architects do, but also as General Electric does in the United States or as all manufacturers do for some or all of their components, so that any manufacturer is more truthfully called an assembler. Selling can be subcontracted to agents; debt collection can be subcontracted for a price; or the whole operation can be franchised, with the originator keeping only the design or the formula as his own.

The contractual organization, in other words, is very familiar to us, although we do not always think of it in this way. It should not, therefore, be very difficult to extend the concept to other parts of the activity or to institutions like schools and hospitals, where it is less familiar, and to apply it to individuals as well as groups.

In a short-term employment contract, people are paid wages, yes, but wages for a particular job for a particular length of time. At present this is seen most often at the top and bottom of organizations. At the top, a chief executive is nowadays hired on a term contract, to do a particular job, and can even have a fee element attached, related to performance and traditionally paid by stock options or bonus, by decision of a review committee. At the bottom, the specific employment contract applies to short-term part-time work, for which people are hired to cover peak loadings—in the summer on farms and vineyards, on Saturdays in supermarkets, and over Christmas in retail stores. There is no long-term commitment by the organization. It is really a fee for a specific piece of work, paid as a wage.

The contractual organization allows individuals or groups to have a relationship with a large organization while still maintaining their independence. It is a way of linking Dionysians and Athenians into the Apollonian center. In some cases, it is, of course, only too easy for the organization to use its superior bargaining power to exploit the individual or the group. People working at home have been notoriously exploited in many industries and trades. That is a problem that we shall examine when we look at the consequences for society. Dionysus does not always spell riches.

Networking

In the early 1980s, Rank Xerox in the United Kingdom needed urgently to cut the cost of its headquarters staff, without losing too much valued expertise.

It came up with a proposal to turn many of its experts into independent professionals and to buy back some of their services for a fixed period of years. Both parties benefited. The organization was able to reduce its employment at senior levels significantly, saving on space, pension contributions, and other related costs. After all, at that time, it was costing $40,000 annually to provide space, food, service, and transport for a senior executive in central London. Xerox was, however, able to buy back much of the expertise it had lost by paying a fee. The individual got a chance to establish himself or herself as an independent, with a guaranteed chunk of business to start with and a benevolent patron at his back.

The organization took great care to make sure that the people to whom it offered this opportunity had the personal qualities and enough self-reliance and technical skill to make a success of independence.

Not everyone is born a Dionysian.

Quality control is the key to the success of the contractual organization. Payment of a fee for work done means that the work done must be the focus of any control. Jaguar Cars pulled itself back to reputation and profitability largely by an attack on the quality of its components, made by subcontractors. The best American companies are obsessed by quality, both of their own end product and of their subcontracted components. McDonalds' beef must be first-rate if its hamburgers are to taste first-rate, and McDonalds do not make the beef.

Quality control, inspections, and examinations sound hierarchical, Apollonian, and antithetical to the Dionysian, Athenian, and Zeus-like values that the contractual organization seeks to satisfy, but they should not be. Checking on results leaves the individual person free to decide on the methods. Control the ends and you can trust others to take care of the means. The Apollonian role culture, conversely, prefers to control the methods, believing that logically, this will guarantee the results. It is cheaper and more liberating to control the results. The contractual organization must be a results-oriented organization, which suits Zeus, Athena, and Dionysus very well.

Two Varieties

Guinness Brewing does not want anyone except Guinness employees making its stout according to its special formula. Only in faraway places like West Africa would Guinness contract it out to licensed brewers. But everything that it makes is sold through other people's stores and bars—it effectively contracts out the contract with the customer.

Marks and Spencer, on the other hand, takes great care to make sure that a well-trained M&S employee is the only person to deal with a customer, but nothing that that employee sells is made by Marks and Spencer; all its manufacturing is subcontracted.

Which is right? Probably both. There is no golden rule.

The Doctrine of Subsidiarity

Contractual organizations believe in subsidiarity, although they may not realize it. The principle of subsidiarity has long been advocated by the Roman Catholic Church, which believes it to be immoral not to push responsibility as far down and out as it will go.

This was restated by Pope Pius XI in Quadragesimo Anno in 1941 as follows: "It is an injustice, a grave evil, and a disturbance of right order for a large and higher organization to arrogate to itself functions that can be performed efficiently by smaller and lower bodies."

It sounds like a condemnation of Apollo.

The Implications for the Managerial Gods

The Erosion of Management

Professionals, self-styled or real, do not like to be "managed," with all that the word today implies about control, manipulation, and direction. They would prefer to use the word *manage* in its colloquial or nineteenth-century meaning, as an equivalent of *coping,* as in "How did you manage today?" or "Did you manage to . . . ?" It is interesting that our old-established institutions or professions do not use the word at all for their *high*-status roles, preferring governors, presidents, directors, senior lecturers, deans, commanders, or even (in the British civil service) secretaries. When the word does occur in such institutions, managers refer to *office managers* or *warehouse managers*—the necessary "coping" roles. Management, in other words, seems to be an Apollonian term. Management began to be a high-status occupation with the rise of the Apollonian corporation some two generations ago.

The first major implication of the new professionalism in organizations, and its Athenian overtones, will undoubtedly be a tendency for "management" to revert to its earlier meaning. In other words, the Apollonian, bureaucratic, administrative part of organizations will become culturally subordinate to the professional parts. Managers will no longer automatically be the high-status people in these organizations.

What, then, must one say about all the planning, organizing, and controlling that is supposed to be the essence of management and on which the organization traditionally depends for its survival? These functions must continue. We must remember, however, that only in the role cultures is there a particular person for every task or role. It is not some equation inherent in nature that a task equals a person. There are many jobs that can be done by temporary groups, and it is a feature of the organizations of consent that the professional members wear a variety of hats, sitting in the morning, perhaps, as the planning group and in the afternoon as the adjudicators on standards—the quality control function. The design and use of the planning, organizing, and control systems will be in the hands of the people whose work is being planned, organized, and controlled, although the actual administration of the systems, the collection and processing of data, could well be done by others. To an Apollonian, it sounds illogical to put the control devices in the hands of those being controlled. To an Athenian or Dionysian, it is insulting and degrading to have it any other way: It would be treating them as children, deviants, or incapable and would start them on the "spiral of distrust."

Adhocracies

One word that has been used to describe the new kind of organization is *adhocracy*.[1] Mintzberg describes it in this way: "Highly organic structure, with little formalisation of behaviour, high horizontal job specialisation, based on formal training; a tendency to group the specialists in functional units for housekeeping purposes, but to deploy them in small market-based project teams to do their work." He goes on: "Of all the configurations, Adhocracy shows the least reverence for the classical principles of management, especially unity of command."[2]

Networks

Nancy Foy sees networks as the key to the new organizations and postulates some laws for their proper management:[3]

1. The effectiveness of a network is inversely proportioned to its goal.
2. A network needs a focus, not a goal.
3. A network needs a spider at the center, not a chairman.
4. A network needs a note or a newsletter, not a journal.
5. A network needs a good list of members more than a set of bylaws.
6. A network needs groups, not committees.
7. A network needs a phone number, not a building.

Both are Athenian structures for Dionysians run by Zeus.

The Need for Leadership

But even though Dionysians and Athenians may be happy to sit in various groups wearing their different hats from time to time, when they are not exercising their professional skills in groups and individually, they are not usually culturally self-sufficient. In practice, they need a Zeus to lead them and Apollonians to serve them.

An examination of the variety of cooperative organizations— ranging from cooperatives of craftsmen, local community redevelopment schemes, and welfare organizations to chemical manufacturing and motorcycle makers—reveals that the successful ones are always *led* by some kind of charismatic energizing figure. He tends to be an unusual Zeus, in that his power seldom stems from ownership but, rather, from personality, ideas, and initiatives—the kind of Zeus that Athenians and Dionysians can accept because his power justifies itself in action, so that he is continually reauthenticating himself in their eyes. Organizations of consent, in other words, have to be led, not managed. Indeed, if one wanted a criticism of our contemporary organized society, it is that it is currently overmanaged and underled. The Zeus of the organization of consent is therefore a critical feature, but he must be one of the gang, different only in his personality, his attitudes, and the way he works, operating with power granted implicitly to him as leader but depending always on his colleagues for their consent.

The Steady-State Village

The organizations of consent and contract still need an administrative steady-state: jobs that must be so prescribed that individuality is squeezed out, regarding which any problems have been solved at the design stage, that is, Apollo's section.

Goods and money must be counted, products and services checked for quality, offices cleaned, computers fed, and machines emptied and filled again. Trains must still run on time and cannot be left to the individual entrepreneurial instinct of the drivers. How are the steady-state sections of our organizations to be run (managed?) under this new cultural revolution?

Apollo, it must now be emphasized, does not disappear in this confrontation of the gods; he only retreats. Individualism and professionalism, with their Athenian or Dionysian attitudes, are widespread, but they *mix* through the other cults and *overlay* them—they do not *displace* them. Just as Zeus, infected by Dionysus, is a more personal Zeus, so Apollo, when infected by Dionysus, becomes a human Apollo. Lots of people, in other words, though craving individual recognition, still have the propensity for order, the liking for discipline and routine in work, and the tidiness of predictability. The New Apollo has a human face.

How is this achieved? Essentially by reducing the size of the Greek temples of each steady-state so that those who work there have names, not just roles, and names that are known to the rest of the organization, and for which the duties attached to each role have meaning, because everyone can see the end result and can understand how his role contributed to the outcome.

In this context, small is not so much beautiful as essential. Without the appropriate scale, Apollo loses his human face, our Dionysian instincts are denied, and the old symptoms of the resistance to Apollo emerge. When Dionysus is denied, his claims and pressures dominate. Once placated, our other cultural instincts can come to the fore. When Apollonians are treated as individuals, they can devote themselves to predictability, and Athenians can spend their time planning, knowing that each is necessary to the other.

It is at this point that we need to change the model to reflect the changing face of Apollo in the organizations of consent. The *village*, with its villagers, must replace the Greek temple as the centerpiece of the organization. Villages are small and personal, and their inhabitants have names, characters, and personalities. What more appropriate concept on which to base our institutions of the future than the ancient organic social unit whose flexibility and strength sustained human society through millennia?

How big, then, might these villages be? It is hard to say, but let us guess that the organizational village would contain a maximum of five hundred working people. Above that number, it is no longer possible to know everyone—anonymity sets in. It is clear that society long ago outgrew the village as far as most of its inhabitants are concerned. And so have many organizations. But it is time to return to it, if we can. Psychologists speak of "environmental disorientation," which can occur when distance or size or complexity becomes too great, so that the individual withdraws from his environment or rebels against it. It is possible that airplanes or ships may become, or have become, so big that people no longer feel safe in them. It is known that some buildings, some conurbations, some institutions, are simply so large that they are repugnant. In one poll, 80 percent of Britons said that they would prefer to live in a village or small town rather than in a large city.

Sir Frederick Catherwood, then head of the British Institute of Management, observed once that the new challenge to management was to find a way of running organizations with "no more than five hundred heads under one roof." It was a call for the organizational village to replace the temples of Apollo.

The Reorganization of Work

The managerial gods cannot be realigned in isolation, however. We have just seen the implications for the size of any steady-state activity, and they go further than that.

Too Big at Sixty-five?

The Urban Church Project in Poplar, London, has been investigating the odd phenomenon that whatever the size of parish, the average core church congregation will level out over time at sixty-five. It also noted that around fifty-five to sixty-five members turned up for their annual meetings and that the average staff of secondary schools had fallen from one hundred to between sixty and seventy. The project began to read and think.

It is widely held, it discovered, that the primary group saturates at 12 members, after which it is difficult to know everybody well. Within a group of 12 there are 66 possible relationships, and within a group of 66 there are 2,145 relationships, which is very close to the point at which any further increase becomes meaningless, that a community becomes a crowd with whom one cannot identify.

The project found that if congregations grew larger than sixty-five members, they would break up into separate groups.

The Harnessing of Technology

In the Apollonian era that is ending, people are the servant of technology. People are hired to operate, service, or often just watch increasingly sophisticated equipment, working in an increasingly advanced technology. The equipment is often so expensive that people must march to its tune, adjust their working day and their habits to it, learn its language, and be in many senses its servants.

This relationship must be reversed if the Dionysian urges of our new workforce are to be satisfied. Technology must once again become the servant of people. Ideology and preaching won't bring this about, of course. But economics will. The cost of providing servants for dominant technologies will, through the exercise of negative power and the hijack, outweigh the economics of scale that originally justified the creation of the technology.

Wherever the professional or craftsman attitude has been dominant—in photography, fashion, science, or farming, for instance—technology has been developed to extend people's capacities. The resulting equipment has remained essentially in the control of one person and his or her assistant. In Apollonian cultures, the technology, for example, the computer or the assembly line, was developed to do as much of the work as possible, leaving people to service the machines and do those bits that the technology could not handle. Craftsmen (Dionysians) need tools, and Apollonians need machines. Although the distinction seems semantic or philosophical, it is not. It is of crucial importance in the future design of the work of our organizations.

The design of technology to extend the capacities of one person or one person and his or her small group of colleagues calls for an advanced rather than a simplified technology. It is easier to design a series of specific machines with people to bring the work to them and to service them than it is to design some all-purpose, robotlike machine tool for the individual craftsman machinist. It is easier to design a large chemical process plant than a small one. Only when the costs of staffing the large one become intolerable will there be economic incentives to design the smaller one. Only when it becomes prohibitively expensive to run an assembly line will we look for ways to automate the line completely and give it to one person to run, or find ways of doing without it.

Economic forces follow human forces as often as not. It is the lag that brings the pains. Wise people anticipate economics, and others react. Which shall we choose?

Flexibility of Work

The organizations of consent and contract prefer that money be paid for work done rather than for time spent. This allows the individual to control his own allocation of time and effort within overall deadlines. The attempts by Apollonian organizations to pay piece rates have always foundered because they confused piece rates with time spent. To couple the two—to determine norms of work for periods of time—must be self-defeating, for it is seen as prescription, control, manipulation, with all the connected overtones disliked by people who might respond to the challenge of fees rather than wages. Any return to contract or piecework must be uncoupled from time spent. There is no inherent reason in many industries why this should not be done. Even in such an Apollonian world as that of life insurance, the salesmen are essentially on contract to be paid, by commission, for work delivered, leaving them free to allocate their own time.

Organizations of consent and contract find it hard to insist that all work be done on their premises. The old tradition of working at home remains with artists, writers, designers, and teachers and is carried over to many consultants, research scientists, and many managers who find it easier and more productive to do some of their work at home or in a place away from the main organization.

Flexitime is but a small and partial step down these roads. Those organizations that have experimented gingerly with flexible working-week arrangements (a set number of hours to be worked in flexible patterns agreed between the individual and his working group) have found no ill effects, but the experiments still deal in minutes or hours rather than days or weeks.

The trend will need to go much further to satisfy the Athenian and Dionysian needs of the new professionalism. There will have to be far more scope for part-time work. Individuals will work for more than one organization simultaneously. Work will be done at home to be brought in at regular intervals or communicated electronically to a central point.

Once again, economics will be the spur. For certain specific (professional) tasks, it will be cheaper to use part-time rather than full-time employees, even after allowing for the extra coordinating time. The possibilities of more part-time or contract work will tap new sources of talent, including the underemployed housewife. The increasing cost of transport to work (reflected ultimately in wages) will make working at home more economically attractive to both individual and organization. The increasing availability of real-time on-line communication links will make it both unnecessary and expensive to have people in one building in order to coordinate them. If people wish to be rewarded with discretionary time (university teachers traditionally spend 20 percent of their time on their own pursuits) instead of money, it may pay the organization to accommodate them, instead of binding them full time to the organization with disproportionate amounts of money.

Existing Athenian organizations (consultancies, laboratories, universities) find that flexibility suits their work flows, which are seldom copy or flow ones. Other work flows must begin to adapt as Apollo retreats. We shall find ourselves investing in the *breakdown* of flow technologies such as assembly lines, but the investment will be justified by economics, not ideology, as the costs of running those flow technologies become prohibitive.

Typists Intrapreneurial

Norman Macrae of *The Economist* is an advocate of more entrepreneurship within organizations and was the first to call it *intrapreneurship*.

He illustrates it thus:

"If you need a typing pool . . . it might be best to set up several competing groups of Typists Intrapreneurial. You would offer an index-linked contract to the group for a set period, specifying the services you wanted in return for a lump-sum monthly payment. The typists would apportion the work amongst themselves, devise their own flexitime, choose their own life-styles, decide whether to replace a leaver by a full-timer or part-timer, or whether to do her work and keep more money per head. They could also decide whether to tender for extra paid work from outside."[4]

A contractual organization at work—with Dionysians led by Zeus?

Self-contained Units

The specialization of work will be reversed in the organizations of consent and contract. Specialization involves the fragmentation of activities and the consequent need for more coordination, systematization, and centralization. With Apollo in retreat, each unit will want increasingly to be given the means of solving its own problems, instead of hitching on to some central procedure. Instead of a central maintenance function, each operating group will want its own maintenance person, to give it more flexibility and self-control. The accounting and sales staff, which have progressively been pulled back into central offices, will begin to be pushed out again. Groups will increasingly be judged by results rather than by methods. To use Norman Macrae's phrase, organizations will be *recompetitioned*. That is, organizations will have more than one unit doing the same kind of work. Those that do it better will provide the models for the others, for competition of this sort sets standards more cheaply and more acceptably than does any central set of rules and checks. Large combines of railways, mines, steel firms, hospitals, and local governments will be divided up again, and although their *areas* of operation might be defined to prevent wasteful competition, they will be allowed the means to secure their own ends. Organizations must then continue to resist the urge to impose the means that succeed in one unit on all the rest or to think that a rationalization of activities will bring the economies it seems to promise.

The truth is that the economies of scale do not follow a constant graph, with economies steadily following scale. Logic and industrial engineering would have it so, but the resistance to Apollo means that after a spurt of economies, increased scale produces diseconomies and the graph flattens out, until eventually the cost per unit actually rises as the cost of operating the controlling systems spirals. Unfortunately, this rise is today concealed by inflation, and in any case, the alternatives are by now lost in history and not comparable, so that, too often, no one notices.

An economist in the Hungarian government once explained to me that even when the economy was centrally planned, they liked to have at least two of every type of plant, even if this principle went against the apparent logic of economics. "It is easier, and cheaper, to let them set standards for each other than for us to try to fix and monitor those standards from the center."

The Successful Cabinetmaker

The cabinetmaker had been very successful. He now had 110 people working for him and had just won a contract with a big chain of retail stores that would more than double his output for the next five years. He saw that he would have to give up his rather informal "village" atmosphere and regroup his people into divisions and hierarchies. While the consultants he had called in were working on the problem, a delegation of his workers came to

him. "We like it the way it is," they said. "We don't want
this factory to grow any bigger. If you want to grow, why
don't you start another factory for this new business?"

And so was the group philosophy born. No factory
had more than 110 workers. A new factory opened every
year, then every five or six months, with 25 percent
growth sustained overall. Each factory made its own line
of products and ran itself, asking the person at the center only for new capital.

But eventually the cabinetmaker had twenty-three
factories. How long could this go on? The pressures
for rationalization were growing stronger. His factories
were beginning to compete with one another for business and to cut their margins (his margins) to beat one
another. The demands for funds were getting progressively larger: He needed more control over cash inflows
if he were to provide cash outflows. The economics of
centralized purchasing of services such as accounting
and advertising were becoming more and more obvious.

And he still wanted to grow. That was his thrill. The
old problem was here again. What should he do? If he
rationalized, he might ruin the whole spirit of the factories, offend his workers and feed opportunity to the
unions, and build up an unwieldy and unwanted central
organization. But could he resist his own need and the
apparent logic of greater consistency and control?

In the end, the cabinetmaker divided his empire. He
no longer has his fingers on each enterprise, only on
three lieutenants. He has lost something, perhaps, but
his organization retains its vigor and its enterprise—and
its inconsistency.

The self-contained unit philosophy must spread to the service
units of organizations. Organizations will increasingly find it
cheaper to contract out many of their central services, such as
their management services, computer bureaus, training departments, and consultancy divisions in engineering, finance, and
advertising. The desire of top management to have all these
activities under their own control conflicts with the needs of the
service groups to be independent, and it eventually conflicts with
the intolerable overhead costs of maintaining them as a free

good for the operating units. There is no reason that these service groups should not be owned by the central organization but not be controlled by it, except in terms of results. Organizations will then find themselves sprouting small entrepreneurs, giving to them freedom under an economic umbrella, ruling by selection and trust rather than procedures and control. Zeus will outrank Apollo.

Organizational Federalism

As Apollo is pushed into retreat and into the "village," the apparent organizational imperatives of increased size and greater consistency will tend to be ignored and indeed reversed: Work flows will be broken up; units will become smaller and more independent; and employees will be working on contract out of sight and hearing. It would, however, be sad to see all the economies of scale and consistency disappear before the march of professionalism. Small may be beautiful and even efficient on its own, but a lot of small, self-centered villages do not necessarily create a great nation. Organizations will rightly try to retain the advantages of coordination and central planning, of copy techniques and specialized inputs, whenever these can be compatible with the new cultural mix of management philosophies.

It would be logical, therefore, to extend the village concept into a form of *federalism*.

Federalism is not just a new word for centralization. Colin Ward (of whom more later) talks of "topless federations" and points to one of the most successful federal operations in the world: the international postal service, through which it is possible to mail a letter in Germany and have it delivered in China. Where, one might ask, is the building of the International Postal Authority? It does not exist. Or who, to take another example, can point to the International Railway Building? It, too, does not exist, yet your ticket can carry you across Europe. Federations can be merely agreements for cooperation.

Yet most federations are more than this. Autonomous entities, usually states or countries, decide to cede certain of their rights to a central federal authority in order to better serve their joint interest. Organizational federalism will probably come about in reverse, by devolution rather than by acts of union, but the net result will need to be the same, a separation of rights and powers between the center and the "villages." The center may retain the ancient rights of shareholders vis-à-vis the villages—that is, the right to a dividend, to the appointment of strategic figures, and to the provision of new strategic finance. There may also be grouped at the center the ancillary services, operating as self-contained units with their own entrepreneurial freedom. No doubt there will, too, be some "federal laws" and a law-enforcing mechanism to ensure a degree of homogeneity among the villages, perhaps on some industrial relations matters, on accounting formulas, on quality procedures. But these would have to be negotiated to ensure that they did not infringe on the independence of the villages or on the requisite variety needed for the long-term survival of the federal organization. Theoretically, the federal center *serves* the states.

The Conditions of Federalism

Derek Sheane identified some of the conditions for "industrial federalism" by comparing the workings of successful federal countries (e.g., the United States or Switzerland) with those of more centralized systems, such as the United Kingdom and France.[5]

Federalism succeeds best when

- There is a common external threat.
- There is a "web of interdependence," so that one state cannot dominate the rest, but each needs the others for some resources.
- There is diversity, with each state having separate needs and looking after its own internal affairs.

Federalism works as long as

- There is a separation of powers.
- There is a clear definition of the roles of these powers.
- There is an inverse relation between the amount of power you give those in authority and their tenure of office.
- The individual is assumed to belong to multiple groups, with a variety of interests.

Federal legislative chambers are usually horseshoe shaped, and there is no "leader of the opposition." The simpler "them and us" polarity has no place in federalism, because life is seen as too complex a business to be dealt with in one dimension.

Villages in a federation would have the freedom to control the means and to negotiate the ends. This is contrary to Apollonian logic, which calculates which means are necessary to its desired ends and then controls those means. In a federation of villages, if one village prefers a three-day week with twelve-hour days and another, a six-hour, six-day week, both would have the freedom to do it their way as long as their output over a particular period was the same. For villages are private territory. Even the landlord cannot enter except by permission or if there is evidence of abuse. As long as the rent is paid and the federal laws are obeyed, independence in a federation is guaranteed.

To permit local idiosyncrasy appears, to an Apollonian, to be lending indulgence to inefficiency. This need not be so. Federalism, unlike corporatism, can exploit the productive spur of competition. In a corporate state, in which *functions* are coordinated, each function must cooperate in order for the whole to work—an invitation to hijack. Concessions to one branch must be matched by concessions to another, which is ruinous competition. Under federalism, the system can be uncoupled. If one village does not cooperate, the whole is not ruined, as there will be other villages that, in return for favors promised or anticipated, will move into the breach. It is a bargaining, not a conflict, situation.

Indeed, if organizations are to avoid the increasing costs of hijack, they will need to uncouple their corporations as quickly as they can. Unions that have become used to exploiting the hijack may be expected to resist the spread of federalism, however, for it will weaken their power.

The professional urges for an individual to leave *his* imprint on *his* work in order to make a difference personally and to work at his own pace and discretion all can be accommodated within a village, by judicious design of the work, because of the flexibility that is possible if all the factors are within one's control. When nothing can be altered without discussion with other units, nothing is altered. In this way, discretion disappears. Zeus organizations remain flexible if they remain independent and small. Gangs came before factories. Factories that are sheds for gangs are more tolerable than factories that are sheds for machines.

Gangs in the Factory: Athenian Villages

In the early 1950s, Standard manufactured the Ferguson tractor in Coventry (England) under license, as well as its own cars, using a "gang" system. An American professor, Seymour Melman, described the process: "In this firm . . . thousands of workers operated virtually without supervision as conventionally understood, and at high productivity: the highest wage in British industry was paid; high-quality products were produced at acceptable prices in highly mechanised plants; the management conducted its affairs at unusually low costs; also, organised workers had a substantial role in production decision-making. In production, the management has been prepared to pay a high wage and to organise production via the gang system, which requires the management to deal with a grouped workforce, rather than with single workers, or with small groups. . . . The operation of integrated plants employing 10,000 production workers did not require the elaborate and costly hallmark of business management."[6]

In the car factory, fifteen gangs ranged in size from fifty to five hundred people, and the tractor factory was organized as one huge gang.

"The gang system sets men's minds free from many worries and enables them to concentrate on the job. It provides a natural frame of security, it gives confidence, shares money equally, uses all degrees of skill without distinction and enables jobs to be allocated to the man or woman best suited to them, the allocation frequently being made by the workers themselves."

Alas, Standard was swallowed up by British Leyland in pursuit of market clout, and Apollo took over from Athena in the factory.

Federal Organizations in Action

Johnson & Johnson is a $10 billion company broken up into 150 independent divisions. Each division is called a *company,* and each is headed by a "chairman of the board." The central staff is small, with no specialists traveling among the subsidiaries. Johnson & Johnson has more than fifty-five consumer product divisions, each responsible for its own marketing, distribution, and research.

Britain's GEC encourages its 130 businesses to retain their own identity. In industrial relations, each business makes its own agreements. Shop stewards, as well as managers, are jealous of their independence and are encouraged to be so. When GEC took over from AEI, the head-quarters' staff was reduced from more than five thousand to under five hundred.

When I called a community school and asked for "the head," the receptionist asked, "Which head?"

The T.I. Group used to advertise itself as a collection of independent businesses in which "we made it big by keeping it small."

Dana's ninety state managers in the United States, contrary to economic logic, each do their own purchasing, have their own cost-accounting system, and control virtually all aspects of personnel policy.

Implications for the Task of Management

No doubt it will be called government, or direction, or anything other than management, but both the center and the villages need to be "run" in these organizations of consent and contract.

The Center

The center will be dominated by planning and by the need to prepare plans, reach agreement on plans, disseminate the plans, and coordinate the village's efforts to implement the plans. The center's aim must be to emphasize the interdependence of the villages, the common threat or purpose of the federation, while recognizing the individual needs of the different villages (Derek Sheane's preconditions for federalism).

The resulting "plan" is not the rational exercise beloved by corporate planners. Rather, it is the balance of forces, the "possible compromise." Both the expectations of the villages and the projects of the center must be accommodated and incorporated into the ultimate jigsaw.

The process, therefore, is one of bargaining, adaptation, persuasion, and compromise. Vision and imagination are required, but so are sensitivity, the ability to understand other points of view, patience, tact, and the skill to weld groups and fuse perceptions. It is a job for Athenians, often led by a Zeus with a dream, a mission, or a vision.

Derek Sheane's mechanisms of federalism will be required to implement the plans. There must be a separation of powers. Those who execute policy must not be exactly the same as those who legislate policy, for this would give too much power to one group. It will be increasingly common in federal organizations to find a two-tier board of policymakers (elected or appointed by various constituencies, for example, the shareholders, the employers, the consumers) sitting above the management team. This is the solution increasingly favored by West Germany (a federal country) and, in principle, advocated by the minority group of industrial leaders in Britain's Bullock Report on Industrial Democracy. Power must be inversely related to tenure of office in a federal constitution, claims Sheane, and policymakers and senior managers will serve for defined terms (the fixed-term contract). Management then is a task for a time, not a career— quite proper to the organizations of consent and contract. There is a clear definition of roles and power. Good fences make good neighbors, and a clear understanding of "boundaries" in work makes it easier to negotiate, plan, and compromise, because expectations become more explicit. Those organizations that depend on contract labor, as in the construction industry, are very specific about expectations of quantity, quality, elapsed time, payment due, and the like—about the *ends* required, but not the *means*. Federal organizations based on villages of consent and contract will need to be equally specific about roles and responsibilities if they are to survive.

Finally, it will be accepted and recognized that an individual person has a variety of interests and can belong to multiple groups. He may be both an accountant and a person with a passion for his region or a product. He may be a devoted citizen of the organization for half the week and a part-time priest for the other half. No group, no organization, should feel able to claim the whole of a person, his time, his energy, and his interests. Nobody can claim a monopoly of other people's loyalty. Again, this federal principle of multiple interests fits neatly into the ideas of consent and contract and the notions of individual freedom.

It will not be an easy place to manage, the center of these minisocieties. The problems will be constantly changing, and so will the composition of the groups to deal with them. The balance of power and of priorities will shift according to the problem and the degree of interest of the various constituencies. Authority will wax and wane for each individual, depending on the expertise for the task in hand and on access to information or to sources of power. Decisions will emerge rather than be made, and it will often be hard to discover where or how they start or finish. A sensitivity to the possible will be more important than an understanding of the ideal. Conflict will be endemic, but if it can be focused on problems and issues rather than on factions or groups of people, it will be managed productively. It is not a place where many would choose or be chosen to work for the whole of their career. People will tend to move in and out of the federal government, staying for perhaps five or ten years at most. Careers at the center will be out. Jobs and roles will be in. For a qualified Athenian, none of this will be frightening or unusual, as it all will fit his needs for variety, flexibility, and mobility and for the politics of persuasion and the art of compromise.

The Truncated Pyramid

Dr. Irving Borwick described the organization ITT Europe as a set of truncated pyramids with a multigon sitting on top of a traditional set of hierarchical organizations. The multigon is made up of product groups, business groups, functions, and associated organizations, which all overlap and interact with one another and sit above and apart from the national ITT companies.

Borwick points out that the nature of authority, influence, power, and conflict changes when moving from pyramid to multigon. In the pyramid, authority depends on position in the hierarchy; influence stems from formal authority; decisions are made at prescribed levels; and

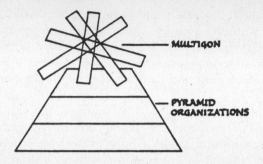

conflicts become established between departments. In the multigon, authority is derived from information and acknowledged expertise. Roles change frequently; decisions are managed rather than made and emerge from groups rather than individuals; and conflict is about problems or situations rather than between departments.

All this, he observed, makes life very confusing if you are moving between pyramid and multigon, as many do. The multigon is a confusing, untidy political world to those from the pyramid.

The multigon seems very much akin to the federal center I am proposing, even if the pyramids are not yet the villages. It is a world for Athenians, not Apollonians.

But what about the federal bureaucracy? Won't that loom large? It should loom, but not large. There is need of an auditing function, an information-collecting mechanism, an accounting and financing operation, and an administrative support to the planning procedures. But they are there to inform, not to control; to serve, not to master.

Detailed assessment and appraisal systems should not be required, for the center will not be responsible for running any community save itself. Financial controls need be minimal, recording only the outcomes and not the details of the methods of each operation. Information will often be particular to a problem or project, rather than routine. It is essential that the bureaucracy see itself as subordinate to, and assisting in, the planning operation. Apollo must be subservient and as small as possible.

The Villages

Common purpose, informality, leadership, individuality, honesty, initiative. All good motherhood words. Words that indicate art rather than science. They are the materials of management in the village.

There are jobs to be done in the organization village, and roles. But the place is too small for careers. To lead is not to manipulate, bribe, cajole, or threaten with promises or fears of future happenings. Effort must come from the desire to play one's part in a common task, to be seen to be doing one's thing and doing it well. Dismissal or layoffs will be exceptional; promotions rare. It must be management by consent and by inspiration. The villages are the heart of the organizations of consent.

There is a checklist for the would-be leaders of these villages—they need leaders, not managers—that goes as follows:

1. *Recognize the Right to Disagree:* In consent organizations, John Stuart Mill's dictum that truth proceeds from argument is widely held. To be invited to disagree is everyone's privilege, but this does not imply that everyone has the right to make the decision. That right belongs to the one on whom the responsibility has been conferred by popular consent. Distinguish discussion from decision wherever possible.

2. *Control by Planning, Not by Checking:* It is legitimate to plan and to replan and to change plans. It is not legitimate to check what others are doing, unless their specific agreement has been obtained. Information for planning is willingly given; information for monitoring less willingly. The manager therefore must work with a variety of planning cycles and must be clearly seen to use past information as a basis for future planning.

3. *Manage by Reciprocal Trust:* Trust and control displace each other. If you are seen to control someone, you are seen not to trust him. If you cannot control him, you must trust him. Similarly, he must trust you. Reciprocal trust is hard to establish and is not self-maintaining. It is easier to trust those whom you have chosen than those whom you are given. Since firing will become impossible with tenure, hiring will become a vital decision in such organizations.

4. *Manage by Platoons:* People find it easier to identify with

smaller groups. Also, the smaller their primary group is, the more that they perceive themselves as having influence. The smaller the group is, the easier it will be to create trust. The concept of platoons (the "ten-group," in Antony Jay's phrase), has served the army, well and must be one of the buttresses in an organization of consent. The platoon concept should be allowed to override other ways of organizing work, which may look more rational but involve larger primary groups. Individuals may be individuals, but they need a group to identify with. Everyone should therefore be a member of at least one platoon.

5. *Be Yourself:* Organizations of consent are personal rather than impersonal. You cannot trust a facade. Openness, frankness, and sincerity are valued. To act a role is to disappear as a person. Whatever your idiosyncracies or habits or values are, let them be visible. Your own sense of identity and purpose gives identity and purpose to your part of the organization. It will be tolerant of unimportant differences, but it will place great emphasis on the concept of "mission" or "purpose."

6. *Husband Your Energy:* Leadership in such organizations is exhausting. To treat individuals as individuals, to welcome disagreement, to tolerate dissent, to listen more than talk, to be true to oneself as well as to others—all require a deal of energy. When energy fails, we fall back on routines and general principles; we listen less and dictate more. Fatigue should not be a battle honor; it should be a crime. Protect what Toffler calls "stability zones," the places of retreat, the times of withdrawal, and you will protect your colleagues.

7. *Think Conceptually:* The ability to find patterns in things, to connect the apparently unconnected, to make the words that shape the vision—this is what distinguishes the statesman from the politician.

8. *Emphasize the Common Task, Purpose, or Output—Not the Separate Roles or Functions.* Tedium, unpleasant effort, and even pain are acceptable in pursuit of a tangible outcome. A job is a job is a bore unless you can see how it matters to the end product. Roles detached from the end result have no soul. Means need to be attached to ends, and the end should be a common purpose signaled by a common language.

This is a checklist for Zeus, a Zeus with wisdom as well as charisma. There will be Apollonians in the villages, looking for security, predictability, and tidiness. There will be Athenians, solving problems with their colleagues. There will be the Dionysian craftsmen and professionals. All will be imbued with the cult of professionalism. They need a Zeus to lead them, to give them common purpose, to recognize their interdependence and their differences.

In Conclusion

We have argued that the tide of resistance to Apollo and bureaucratic corporatism cannot be halted. In an economy of plenty, individualism will flourish. To tamper with the organizations of Apollo through job redesign or to soften the blow with promises of job security and participation will not make these corporate prisons any easier for the individualist. Apollo must retreat. We must find ways of designing and running organizations in which the other gods predominate and in which Apollo is encouraged to have a human and a smiling face. If bigness and consistency force an inhuman Apollo on us, then bigness and consistency must be reduced.

Will it happen?

It is happening. In Britain, three-quarters of the member firms of the Confederation of British Industries employ fewer than two hundred people. In Germany, the proportion is higher still. It is not in these organizations that the strikes and absenteeism occur. In 1966 the British Donovan Commission on Industrial Relations found that even in unionized small firms, only 25 percent of the managers had ever experienced a strike, compared with 43 percent in large plants.

In most countries, the construction industry provides an interesting example of an existing federation of villages at work. It is a structure that grew out of the nature of their work and their technology. Each job must be treated differently, so that consistency must be left to the lowest common denominators. Subcontracting is an accepted principle of the work. Groups of "professionals" (artisans, experts, or specialists) work together on site under the leadership of someone who, to be successful, must be an accepted Zeus figure. The functions of the center are, perforce, limited to obtaining new projects, selecting key staff, counting and collecting the money, and providing a few advisory services. Attempts to rationalize the construction industry, to make it more Apollonian and predictable through "industrialized building" techniques, failed to have their expected impact. The nature of the work does not suit Apollo. The list of subcontractors posted on a building site is the "organigram" of an organization of contract.

Federations of villages and the accompanying managerial cultures were thrust on the construction industry. Its companies were, in a sense, fortunate. Other industries and other organizations must follow by deliberate decision in place of instinctive reaction. We shall have to change our work flows, for we cannot wait for them to change us.

There is, however, a certain inevitability about all this. Large, nonfederalized Apollonian systems are likely to self-destruct after a time if they do not change. But all will not then disappear. The work will remain, for it is the bureaucracy surrounding it that will go. Phoenix-like, new villages will emerge from the ashes of the Greek temples. Society will continue, but only after trauma and confusion. It would be preferable to avoid them by both conscious thought and deliberate action.

In Germany, Scandinavia, and France, the trend toward larger organizations has slowed down and, in some cases, has reversed. In Britain, size and consistency still seduce. Britain is thus being forced to confront the Apollonian dilemma more urgently and more dramatically than others. The developments of the next ten years will be watched with great interest by other countries. No doubt, with their puritan zeal, the British will publicize the traumas and not the successes, but there are bound to be some of both.

This is a conflict that has been long heralded by some, even if ignored by most. In 1951, Lord Radcliffe, an eminent British jurist, gave the annual series of BBC Reith Lectures, in which he remarked, "The British have formed the habit of praising their institutions, which are sometimes inept, and of ignoring their character, which is sometimes superb. In the end, they will be in danger of losing their character altogether and being left with their institutions—a result disastrous indeed."

Villages Rule OK

In the past, Britain's industrial organizations may not have performed as well as they should have, but Britain is famous for many things: for the excellence of its theater, television programs and journalism; for agriculture, consulting, and financial services; for university education and research; for exploration and mountain climbing. When you think about it, all these activities are based on small groups, professionals, and strong leaders: Athena, Dionysus, and Zeus.

Italy has now a thriving textile industry. One of its governments exempted firms with fewer than twenty workers from all bureaucratic controls. As a result, of the fifteen thousand textile factories in Tuscany, thirteen thousand have fewer than ten employees. The industry has now just about the highest textile wages in the world. Textile villages.

"Keep it simple, stupid" (KISS) has long been a watchword of American business. Today it is "keep it small and simple," with all organizational observers advocating a return to small comprehensive units that can influence their own destiny and therefore that of the corporation as a whole. Change and innovation, they observe, come from villages led by Zeus.

8

The Consequences

The gods are changing. Organizations are restructuring and re-balancing to stay alive. It is happening, let us be clear, out of self-interest and a survival instinct, not because there is some grand vision for society or even some new theory of management that has caught the imagination. We are stumbling backward into the future, a typically British posture that allows us to look longingly toward a receding past while actually adapting to the future. Unheralded and unwittingly, our organizations are shaping a new society, because these new arrangements are not just the stuff of business: Their logic, and eventually their appeal, will catch on everywhere, in all organizations.

Just think of it. Schools need not be the total institutions that they have always been. So much of what they do could be done elsewhere and by others. Computers in the home will be more effective than textbooks; work experience turns out to be an excellent way of learning social and technical skills (should we be surprised?); children learn best with adults, and adults learn, too, when cast as coaches or teachers. The open university, pioneered in Britain and now imitated across the world, is not only a distance-learning venture; it is also an example of a contractual organization (paying fees to writers, producers, and tutors) with a professional core and a federal structure. Fascinated by the

The Affluent Outworker

university's technological innovations, the world has not yet grasped the organizational innovations, but they provide the beginnings of a model for the other parts of education. If each school were the core of an educational network for all ages in its own community, there would be few lives in that community untouched, if only because more education would take place in the home.

And if schools, why not hospitals? To some extent, hospitals are already becoming the physical hub of a substantial network, with many ancillary services contracted out; more equipment on loan to individuals but "plugged in" to the hospital; more care and help offered by associated services—the Regional Health Authorities of Britain are really federal organizations, although they are, most of them, still managed as if they were Apollonian entities.

Or take fees and their implications. More people paid on a fee basis means that more people will be able to decide where and when to do their work. The nine-to-five office routine, the daily commute, and the home used as a hotel are not the lot of most people on a fee basis. Yes, they must be part of a network or of several networks. Many will do most of their work for only one or only a few large organizations. But they can connect with those networks or organizations by telephone and television, as well as by personal visits. More people will work *from* home if not *at* home, using their home as their base, as farmers and sales representatives have always done. This change in work patterns will not leave the home and its routines unaffected.

Professional organizations and fee-based earnings rely on qualifications and certificates to get started. It will be increasingly hard to get a job or a contract without some piece of paper to prove that you are competent. In the end, the results may speak for themselves, but to start with, the paper must do part of the selling. A more Dionysian society heralds a credential society, suggesting the need for education throughout life, retraining, and updating. Without qualifications and a professional network, the individual will be trapped in one of the new organizational villages, which, however well they are led and managed, will feel like prisons to some. Credentials and a network are the passports to leave as well as the permits to enter.

That is fine for those who can get credentials, but what happens to the rest in these professional, contractual organizations made for Athenians and Dionysians? The British census of population in 1981 revealed that the numbers of unskilled manual workers in manufacturing had fallen by 46.2 percent and semiskilled by 22.6 percent, whereas employers and managers had risen up by 18.6 percent and account workers by 16.0 percent. The unskilled and the semiskilled are not wanted, so what are they going to live on or do? Is more unemployment an inevitable outcome of the more professional, contractual organization?

And women? In the last twenty years the number of working wives in Britain has grown faster than the number of men out of work. It is not that women are displacing men in their jobs but that the new businesses and the new organizations want more part-time, short-term, semicontractual workers, semiskilled but reliable. Women fill the bill more easily than men do, who still hanker after the permanent job with some sort of long-term career structure. The new structures and the new jobs may be insecure and many of them poorly paid, but they fit into the flexilives of many women, allowing them to be mothers and home managers as well as workers. Among the semiskilled the term *house husband* may become more common. Among the professionals, will women get their share of the jobs?

Perhaps enough has been said to demonstrate that the reordering of the gods and the redesign of our organizations will make a difference in the way most people live and in the way society functions. Because organizations provide the skeleton of society, any change in their ways will affect all of us, whether we approve or lament. In this chapter, we look at the three major consequences for society: the decline of the employment society, the new ownership, and the new paradigms. Each of them offers exciting opportunities, but they also give rise to the new questions.

The questions may be old ones like What will we live on? or How will we learn? but they will require new answers in a reorganized society. If we don't try to answer them, we may be facing the way Rome faced at the start of its decline.

The Decline of Rome (and Britain?)

Gordon Rattray Taylor's list of the symptoms of Rome's decline has disturbing echoes in several Western countries today:[1]

1. The breakup of small-scale farming, leading to urbanization and the formation of a "mass society," with massive immigration as a further factor causing cultural disintegration.

2. The breakup of the empire and the development of an adverse trade balance.

3. The issue of doles and benefits to the urban masses and their growing preoccupation with conflict and violence.

4. The passing of power to the prime functional group, the army (or, for us, the trade unions?) and their irresponsible use of this power.

5. The breakup of the aristocracy under middle-class expansion, followed by the destruction of the middle class in the interests of the lower classes.

6. A continuously escalating inflation and even heavier taxation to support the constant increase of army pay and social services.

7. The decline of public safety as armed bands, drawn from the middle classes as well as the masses, seek to make a living outside society.

8. In place of the lower classes, modeling themselves on higher ones, the process is revised, and popular manners, dress, and so forth are imitated.

9. The growth of superstition, belief in astrology and other occult systems, and the turning toward prospects of bliss in another world.

10. The imposition of a wealth tax, followed by the confiscation of property.

11. The steady mounting of external threats: food supplies becoming unreliable because of irrigation failures, soil erosion, and the Third World's desire to keep its products for itself.

12. A reign of terror, in which spying, denunciation, and torture are employed.

13. The decline of artistic and technical greatness.

14. Corruption and intrigue at unprecedented levels.

There is still time to escape the full list.

The Decline of the Employment Society

It may be as odd now to talk of employees as it already is to talk of servants. Yet only two generations ago, domestic service was one of the main categories of work. There was an "upstairs" and a "downstairs" in most middle-class homes. There are still cooks and gardeners, of course, but today we call them caterers and garden maintenance firms, because if you think about it, the middle-class family is now automated and contractual. The same work is done, but not by servants.

Already in the United States today, almost half of all adults of working age are *not* in full-time employment. No, they are not all unemployed, although too many are. Many are still in education, some are self-employed, more are employed part time, and both of those categories are going up while the rest are what the OECD quaintly but correctly calls "unpaid domestic workers." Together, these categories add up to 47 percent of the total. It will take another generation perhaps, but the numbers of those prepared to call themselves "employees"—as opposed to "independents," "consultants," "partners," "associates," or "members"—will steadily diminish until they are in a definite minority. It may sound like playing with words, but new words are the heralds of change: They symbolize a significant change in the relationship of individual to organization, and they sound some kind of death knell for the employment society as we knew it.

The employment society was a convenient idea—by guaranteeing a job to everyone who wanted one, society provided money, structure, and identity to every household. Call it a form of social control if you want to, employment was certainly the thing that held society together and made it work. Social welfare could then be the insurance that it was intended to be, a fallback for the temporarily unfortunate. So pervasive has the idea of employment become that "work" effectively means "a job," and a person without employment passes into an empty space in society, without income, without status, without occupation—without anything, as Shakespeare said of old age.

It is fashionable to blame unemployment on new technology, and there are those who hope that the lapse from full employment is only temporary, that the new technologies will grow new jobs, and that we shall return before long to the employment society in all its Apollonian splendor. The truth is probably more subtle and more complicated. Yes, indeed we are seeing, and will see more of, the phasing out of old ways and old industries and the birth of new ones. This inevitably causes a lot of human displacement. But the new businesses and the new occupations require brains rather than brawn: fingers, not muscles. This is not just a difficult retraining problem; it actually signals the need for a different sort of organization to cope with different requirements and different sorts of people. The days of the factory that dominated the town are gone forever. To put it simplistically, the new technologies need Dionysians and Athenians, not Apollonians, as their main resource, and they, as we have seen, require a looser sort of organization.

Tomorrow's Office Today?

LSI Logic, in Silicon Valley, California, under Wolf Corrigan, gave *The Economist* a vision of the workplace of the future.[2] There is one huge room shared by administrative and management people. No private offices, but private meeting rooms. It is an almost paper-free office, people gleaning information from computer terminals or neighbors. The place is eerily quiet, although there are more than four hundred employees, but each professional working there has more than $100,000 of computing power to back him up. LSI Logic estimates that because of this equipment, each circuit designer is producing four times as many designs, with greater reliability, than would have been possible only three years earlier.

The results for employment? Wolf Corrigan saw two types of jobs disappearing—the less skilled ones in manufacturing and servicing and the jobs of the middle manager. Any manager, he reckoned, should be as technically skilled as his few subordinates if he wants to keep on working.

The New Jobs

In ten years, the United States created 19 million new jobs: 5 percent in manufacturing, 11 percent in goods-producing industries, 12 percent in the traditional service sector, and 72 percent in the information sector (teachers, accountants, bankers, insurance brokers, lawyers, computer programmers, and other people who process bits of information or move them about).

The twenty-hour week is becoming more common as the proportion of part-time workers grows in all countries. Much of this new work goes to women, and much of it is in services in which the work has sharp peaks that require extra staff at irregular intervals. Part-time work suits the services and it often suits women, who can combine it with household and child management. As a result, the proportion of women in work in the OECD's biggest economics rose from 50.5 percent in 1975 to 60.4 percent in 1993.

Truncated Careers

To put it another way, the organizations of the new technologies will find it more economic to pay fees rather than wages to many of these new workers, whom they will require more intermittently and can manage by more remote control. The contractual fringe of the new organizations is likely to be large. Why employ someone all week when you really need only two days of her creative talent or dexterity?

But some will still be employed, and in central and local government, schools, hospitals, and prisons, it is likely to be the majority. In others, it will be only the professional core. Employment, however, is likely, even for them, to last for fewer years than it used to. A smaller, flatter organization needs more people to leave it sooner, to provide promotion opportunities for those behind. The new organizations are likely to follow the armed services in stipulating varying lengths of service, from three to twenty years, to be reviewed at the discretion of the organization, not the individual. Tenure in universities, the professions, and business, will increasingly have a terminal date that will bring it closer to twenty-five years than the current forty-eight. Even for the professional core, in other words, employment will be only a phase of life, not much longer than the educational phase. Maybe the French are right in talking of the three ages of man— the age of learning, the age of working, and the age of living. Maybe it will be as rare to hear someone in his sixties talk of his

employment days as it would be to hear them talk of his school-
days. Both would be phases of the past, a fount of memories,
reminiscences, and stories, but something left behind.

In practical terms, organizations will follow the universities in
treating tenure for life as a rare and precious privilege. There
will be more service contracts at all levels, more short-term appointments for two or three years to a particular project or team
(as already happens in research groups and in nonprofit organizations). More appointments will be subject to review after five
or seven years. Early retirement will become the norm rather
than the exception for the expensive people—top management
and specialists. It will be done in the interests of economy and
efficiency and to prevent the organization's becoming an elderly
ghetto or a gerontocracy, but the end result will be to limit employment to the middle years of life for most people.

The 50,000-Hour Job?

It used to be that people worked for 47 hours a week
(including overtime), for 47 weeks, for 47 years of their
life. Multiplied out, that comes to just over 100,000
hours of employment in a lifetime.

Times are changing. The 35-hour week is common in
many offices. What with public holidays, sick leave, absenteeism, and paid leave, many people now have 10
weeks or more away from the organization, leaving 42
weeks of work a year. A graduate may not start work
until he or she is twenty-three or twenty-four and will
often plan to leave before sixty, giving 35 years of active
working life. That multiplies out to just over 50,000
hours in a lifetime.

We shall soon have halved the lifetime job. We shall
have spent the gains of productivity on reducing employment, in hours and days and years.

The 50,000-hour job may not happen in the same way for all
people. Some will take their hours in an intensive period of
twenty years, working all the hours that they can find and then
moving on, in midlife, to other pursuits. Others will spread it
thinly, working part time for many years. Others will chunk it,
interleaving periods in a job with periods in education, child

rearing, or caring for their elders. Whatever form it comes in, a 50,000-hour employment life signals a lot of life beyond employment, a lot of time when every individual will define himself or herself in ways that have nothing to do with being employed in an organization.

Life Beyond Employment

What will they be doing? They will be unofficially employed or, as they would say, busy with other things. Work, with odd lags and sags, expands to fill the space available for it, much of it going to build up the unofficial or informal economy. People will use their new discretionary time to make more money in the black economy, to save money by doing for themselves what they used to pay others to do for them (the household economy), or to save other people money by doing things for them for free (the volunteer economy). It all is work, and some of it is paid for, but none of it is called employment. It is a world for small Zeus figures, private Dionysians, and illicit Athenians. There will also be those, sadly, who do nothing, who find it hard to live without the structure of employment as well as its money, who need the traction of employment to pull them out of bed in the morning: Apollonians bereft of a temple. For them, the decline of the employment society is all bad news.

The Informal Economies

The Inland Revenue in Britain (like the Internal Revenue Service in the United States) estimated that something like 7.5 percent of the country's taxable income was not declared and was illegal. This would mean that the average household spent something approaching $1,600 in the black economy. Other estimates ranged from half that to almost double. In Italy, some think that this amount might be as much as 20 percent of GNP, with many small businesses and self-employed people invisible to the state, and in eastern Europe this amount might even reach 30 percent.

The completely legal household economy is difficult to value. How does one calculate the rearing of children, the growing of potatoes, or the cleaning of houses? The best way to do it is instead to count the hours of labor. One such estimate calculated the figure for the United Kingdom to be 51 percent of all the hours worked.[3]

Employment is going out of fashion because Apollonian organizations, like middle-class families after World War II, are automating and contracting out. As with the middle-class families, the work is still there to be done, along with some new and different work, but it will be done in new ways and in new kinds of organizations. It is a change of gods, triggered by structural changes in economic life and by new technology, but far reaching in the way it will affect the whole bone structure of what used to be the industrial society. Whether we like it or not, more and more of us will have to follow Zeus and Dionysus for more and more of our lives. Apollo's temples, which have offered some sort of sanctuary to so many for so long, will not disappear—the new organizations must be as tightly regulated as they are loosely structured—but they will be smaller and lower, with less room in them and more selection regarding both entry and exit. Even the people in these smaller temples may no longer think of themselves as employees, as we shall see.

The New Ownership

Sheer size and the complexity, inflexibility, and accumulating slack that result from size are key factors in the flight from Apollo. But so is the reluctance to be owned by another, even if the pay is good. Marx was right—to be another's wage slave is wrong; it is alienating, ultimately humiliating, and a denial of one's full freedom. No one wants to be a "human resource" (the cold language of Apollonian organizations), no matter how well remunerated, if there is another choice. Marx was also right in seeing that when capital and labor were in separate hands, there was inevitably conflict between the two, a conflict that in the end capital would always win, no matter how well protected labor was. In the end, capital expands by using as little labor as it can as productively as it may. That makes a lot of sense if you are the owner of the capital or the agent of the owners, but it makes much less sense if you are part of the "as little labor as possible."

The small businessman understands the problem in his gut. He knows that if he wants to build up the business, at the outset he has to work all the hours he can for as little money as he can live on, to build up the assets, the goodwill, and the turnover of the business. A good salary comes later. Even then, with a thriving business in hand, he knows that if he wants to grow richer, he must pay himself poorly but let the business grow. He can make the trade-off because he is both capital and labor in one. The small farmer can make and understand a similar trade-off, because he too provides the capital and the labor himself. It is when they both grow bigger and employ extra help that capital and labor are divorced, and as in all divorces, arguments break out over the division of the property.

The employment organizations that grew up under industrialization magnified and formalized that divorce. The only way in which employees could benefit from a growth of capital was to ask for more wages. These were naturally resisted because they detracted from the growth of capital unless they could in some way be tied into even greater productivity. The adversary system of management and unions was born of the divorce between capital and labor.

One interesting outcome of the gradual decline of employment and the rise of new forms of organization may be a reconciliation of capital and labor. Dionysians do not like to be managed, or owned, by anyone. Not only, therefore, do they look for organizations of consent, in which they have a right of veto on any important decisions; they also look for organizations that in some way or other are "theirs," not "other people's." Professionals work by choice in partnerships, in which capital increases belong to the partners. If formal partnerships are impossible, then universities, schools, hospitals, churches, and volunteer bodies are at least non-profit-making organizations, which means, in effect, that any surplus earned is put back into the organization, to be spent, invested, or given away with the consent of the members.

The Dionysian swell is likely, therefore, to result in more and more requests and demands by people in organizations for a share in the fruits of ownership as well as the fruits of labor. Even those remaining in the Apollonian centers of the new federal organizations will see themselves as professional staff, not as employees. At the top management level, there are already share-option schemes in more and more businesses. Common in America, these schemes became really tax efficient only after 1980 in Britain and are now growing rapidly. It is an obvious way in which to marry labor and capital, with the result that top managers do not, in those firms, usually think of themselves as employees but instead as co-owners, partners, or members of the corporation.

Why stop at top management? Why can't everyone have a share of the spoils?

In 1975 there were only thirty employee share schemes in Britain. There are now more than six thousand, involving 1.5 million workers. That is a start, but it is still less than 10 percent of all those employed in industry or commerce. Furthermore, many of those schemes are discretionary; that is, a bonus is declared at the discretion of the board, making it look like benevolence rather than one's rightful share in the capital. The pressures are bound to grow.

It is, after all, only ownership that really counts. What you own you don't destroy or even kick. We don't break up the televisions, washing machines, and other household automata that have revolutionized our homes, because they are *ours*. People, on the other hand, have been known to kill the goose that lays the golden egg if it is laying those eggs for others but not for them. We shall have to find more ways by which those who work in organizations receive a direct financial benefit from the growth of capital. When that happens, technological change, which may cut labor but will increase the worth and value of the organization, will be welcomed by people who are both sides of the coin at once, owners are well as workers.

Shares in the Stock

The new ownership will come in many forms. Most obviously and perhaps most powerfully, it will come as a share in the stock of a business. Why couldn't a monthly paycheck be part salary and part stock? If this is as yet too fanciful, we shall certainly see more new businesses rewarding their founder-members with shares in their joint creation, a recognition that whereas some will have contributed money, others will have provided expertise and specialized skills or just sheer hard work. Companies going public for the first time will increasingly offer their shares at a discount to those who work for them, and when they shed bits of their business, the new trend of buyouts provides a way for the workers to take on board the responsibility and the risk of owning a bit of their own business at a price that is low, to reflect the risk, but therefore within their reach.

Cooperatives

The extreme form of share ownership is a full cooperative, in which all the members of the cooperative are owners. Because ownership is totally vested in the workers, they think of themselves as "members" and not as "employees." The marriage of capital and labor is complete. Ironically, however, since cooperatives started as a reaction against capitalism, they have always tended to reject the growth of their capital as a form of reward, calling profit *surplus* and taking their rewards in the form of larger wages, dividends, or bonuses. Partly, therefore, because of their ideological dislike of capital, many cooperatives have always been financially undernourished, without the resources to survive troughs and depressions, or the investment to take advantage of new markets or new technologies. By denying themselves the motives of their former users, the cooperatives are not only being irrational, but they are also being naive and self-defeating, given that they operate in capitalist market economies. It is not capital, after all, that has been at fault, but the way it was used by some at the expense of others. Happily, there are signs—in Italy and France, particularly—that the cooperative movement is coming to terms with reality.

Italy Cooperates

At last count, there were almost four thousand cooperatives in Italy, many of them in building construction, with fewer members in services and industrial production.[4] It is said that only 5 percent of the cooperatives die each year, whereas as many as 25 percent new ones are formed.

Financially fragile, they have improved their competitiveness by bonding together in consortia to compete for larger tenders and orders, which allows them to act big while staying small. They have also kept management to a minimum (cooperative law says that there should be only one white collar for every twelve blue collars) and have used their federations to help raise money and to put pressure on the state and the banks to provide loans. The state, indeed, has been very supportive, passing laws in 1951, 1963, and 1978 to give specialist status to cooperatives and to provide cheap capital. Idealism is strong among the cooperatives, but today in Italy it is tempered by realism. As a result, cooperatives are now an important third sector in the economy.

Trusteeship

Third, ownership can take a more constitutional form, with workers becoming the formal owners of the organization but with that ownership expressed collectively through a trust, which owns the company on behalf of the workers. Or as in Britain's John Lewis Partnership, the workers can be the titular owners of the company but delegate their powers to an elected council. In these cases, capital seems to be not so much married to labor as put in trust for it, to be used on its behalf. It feels like ownership by remote control and is less compelling to the individual than a direct share in the organization's assets.

The Scott Bader Commonwealth

Ernest Bader was a dynamic Swiss businessman of strong Christian convictions who went to Britain, settled there, and built up a thriving business. In the 1950s, he started to hand over the business to his workers, although he remained chairman. The shares of the business (Scott Bader Company Limited) are now wholly owned by the Scott Bader Commonwealth, a trust, on behalf of the employees. His hope was that by this means capital and labor could be reunited, giving more meaning to work, more responsibility for their destiny to the workers, and removing any sense of exploitation by the owners. An array of democratic mechanisms was set up at the same time to allow the workers, now also members of the commonwealth, to express their views regarding the management of the company, including four directorships on the company board.

Does it work? "To a degree" would perhaps be the best answer. No one at Scott Bader feels owned by anyone else, but they do not feel that they own the place, either. Ownership vested in the commonwealth and not in individual shares has somehow been put into quarantine—it won't contaminate, but you can't get at it.

Representation

Fourth, ownership can be expressed by representation. When it is impossible, as in the state corporations or state services, to have a share in the capital or when it is difficult and perhaps meaningless because miniscule, as in very large business operations, at least some ways can and should be found to give the employee some say in the way that the capital is used. Representative democracy as the way to enfranchising the worker has been favored by managements, by governments, and by the European Union. Some would do it with worker directors, and some by works councils or by more bottom-line participation in the day-to-day decisions of management. It is perhaps the only way for employees to exert some control over their own destinies and to share in the future of their organization if capital is inviolate. The trouble is that no one seems to want it very much, perhaps because they realize that it is a mere shadow of the real thing.

Workers and Democracy

A survey of workers' attitudes toward more representation and say in their companies produced the following results:[5]

Only 4 percent of employees specify "campaigning to get employees on the board of directors" as a priority for trade unions.

Only 10 percent of employees mention "workers having seats on the board of directors" as one of the four things they would most like to achieve.

Only 17 percent mention "getting employees a bigger say in running the organization they work for" as being an important objective for trade unions.

Only 8 percent think it is important for workers to have a bigger say in management's decisions about finance and investment.

Only 20 percent think it is important for workers to have a bigger say in the day-to-day running of the company they work for.

Only 3 percent think it is important for union officials to have seats on the board of directors.

In the large corporations of state and private enterprises, in local government and the state services, the employee culture will remain ingrained. There seems no real possibility in these organizations for capital to be married to labor. We may, however, expect the feelings of professionalism to be increasingly expressed in a right to be consulted, not through representative democracy, but directly. These places will have to lean over backward to become organizations of consent, precisely because they cannot turn their workers into owners. Representation, however, is not the easiest or best way to do it, whereas direct democracy requires small units—in which everyone can, if need be, be fitted into one room or one shed—federally linked. If Dionysians cannot be partners, they at least want the right to shout no and to shout it themselves.

A share in the ownership of the organization will always remain the best way to keep one's freedom in that organization. Dionysians and Athenians will, we may be sure, be looking for more ownership to replace their dependence on the Apollonian structure. If they cannot get ownership, then the right to be consulted, personally, will become more pressing; in other words, organizations must become smaller until the individual, and not his or her representative, can be heard at the top.

The New Paradigms

Paradigm is a word made fashionable by T. S. Kuhn, writing about the way that science advances. A paradigm is essentially a set of assumptions: Change the set and you change the view. A whole new way of looking at things can release new insights and new energies. When Copernicus suggested that instead of the sun's encircling the earth, the earth and other planets were going around the sun, he did not actually change anything except the way we saw things, but he did set science on a new course.

Similarly, new sets of assumptions about people, work, and organizations will put society on a new course. It may be a chicken-and-egg process—difficult to say which at any time is cause and which is effect—because organizations are so entwined in daily life and daily values, but it is less important to be able to say what started it than to be clear what "it" is that has changed.

The Feminine Strain

The changing role and status of women is a good example of the chicken-and-egg syndrome. It is not the Apollonian crisis that has caused the women's liberation movement or the other way around, but the move toward more task and person cultures that has definitely made it easier for women to become properly involved in organizations, at the top and in the middle as well as at the bottom. The pressure in society at large for women to have the same career and work opportunities as men has allowed a more feminine strain to infiltrate organizations. It is appropriately symbolic that Athena is a goddess, whereas Dionysus was the favored god of those who might be called the liberated women of ancient times.

The feminine strain shows itself not just in the physical presence of more women but also in a heightened awareness of creativity, sensitivity, personal relationships and feelings, personal worth, and individual differences. Men care about these things, too, of course, some of them more than some women do, but a predominantly male culture will keep such things under cover and control and will promote toughness, discipline, and impersonality. The feminine strain is more noticeable in the Athenian and Dionysian cultures, and the male characteristics are revealed more in Zeus and Apollo.

The more Athenian or Dionysian an organization is, therefore, the greater the feminine strain will be, and the easier it will be for women to have a proportionate influence. Advertising agencies, market research firms, television production teams, schools, hospitals, and law courts all are arenas where women are increasingly prominent, even if they had to fight hard at first to overcome the male control of some Dionysian strongholds, as in the law courts or the hospitals. Apollonian and Zeus organizations, however, remain predominantly male in sex and attitude, as the composition of the boards of most European industrial companies reminds us—hardly a female name on any of them. The decline of Apollo must be, therefore, an opportunity for women.

So, as we have seen, is the growth of the contractual organization. No doubt much of the work is semiskilled, irregular in hours, and poorly paid, but the evidence is that although it could be better, it is better than nothing and better, for many women, than full-time employment, which leaves no time for anything else. The employment of women has actually risen in all European countries while the unemployment of men has been accelerating.

The results are often exciting though often confusing. Work roles in households become reversed, blended, or confused. Women may find it easier to take on new work roles but still difficult to unload the caring and homemaking roles, partly because men may not want them, partly because women may want to hang on to them. Men, it seems, like vacuuming, doing laundry, and cooking (the proactive tasks) but are less crazy about dusting and child care. How does a woman decide when to leave career for motherhood, even if only temporarily? Should men also be expected to give up their careers for a period of child rearing? Do husbands accompany their wives to their official functions when the male officials have their wives by their side, or is a woman's work something she does on her own, often under her maiden name? Does the language of "and partner" rather than "and wife," which more and more official invitations now use, tell us something about the emergence of the feminine strain or only confirm the fragility of marriage? These are some new questions for a society that is having to work with a new paradigm of women. That paradigm does not treat women as men, which would be merely perpetuating the old paradigm, but relaxes the entry restrictions giving permission to women to act like men. The new paradigm treats women as different but as good as men, with their own talents, gifts, and particular needs. It is an exciting paradigm, offering chances to both men and women to develop more aspects of themselves, to explore new roles, and to form new relationships. It offers an escape from stereotyping, from the forced dependency of female on male, and the possibility of more partnerships of equals—proper Dionysian pairings. It is happening, in part, because the changing cultures of our organizations allow it to happen. In Japan's Apollonian world, however, women are still seen as the home and family managers for their men.

Confusing Paradigms

I work from home and at home. My wife helps with my correspondence, does the typing, answers the telephone, and manages my appointments—much as a secretary would, in fact, and she is paid accordingly.

She used to answer the phone by giving her name, thereby identifying herself as one of the family. This seemed to embarrass and confuse many callers, who still think of work being done in office or factory or shop and see home as a private sanctuary—"Oh, I'm sorry to bother you," they would say, "I'll call some other time."

She then took to answering the phone during normal office hours as "Charles Handy's secretary." This worked beautifully for all those calling from an office, often secretaries themselves, but it caused anger among some women friends who called. "How demeaning," they said, "how could you put yourself down like that? Why don't you use your own name? You are a person, aren't you, not a piece of property?"

You really need to know whether it's an Apollonian or a Dionysian calling before you answer the telephone!

The Credential Society

It will be a more flexible world. People will move jobs more often because jobs will be shorter. They may work part time or be self-employed, for two or more organizations at once. Many will turn their hobby or their profession into a tiny business on the side, and others will be forced into self-employment as a positive alternative to unemployment. Offices will be the focal points of networks, with many people telecommunicating (by telephone or computer) much of the time, traveling to meetings when need be. Offices and shops will increasingly be on the fringe of cities rather than in the middle, in order to enlarge their catchment areas, and more homes will turn the garage or the back room into a study or a workshop. Time, for most people, will be more discretionary, up to them how to use it. Although many people will probably choose to use it to do more work to make more money, some will delve deeper into self-sufficiency or community work. It will be a more flexilife world, with fewer people able to define themselves, Apollonian style, as a GM man or a GE woman.

Isochrones

Draw a line on a road map to mark how far you could travel by car, rail, or bus from your home in an hour. You have now drawn an *isochrone,* which is like a contour on a map, except that it joins points that are the same distance away in *time,* not the same height.

If you live on the edge of a city, your isochrones will be very jagged, taking you perhaps twelve miles into the center of the city in one direction or sixty miles in another. Add in airplanes and it becomes even more jagged.

Freeways and beltways create a lot of distance in isochrones. The big beltway around London will eventually pull London's center of gravity outward when people realize that the isochrones for an office on the beltway are much bigger than for one in the center of the city, giving it a much bigger catchment area.

Empty commuter trains, perhaps?

Flexilife sounds fun, and it can be. People will end up with portfolios of work rather than one occupation that saw them through life. Instead of having to obtain money, status, and fulfilment from one job, they can be shared a bit among different parts of work and life, with money coming from perhaps one activity but status from something that provides little financial reward. It will be a more Dionysian world.

It will also be a more insecure world. Dionysians obtain security from their professionalism. A doctor is, as long as he stays within the law, always a doctor. She or he might not be a good doctor, but even bad doctors can still practice. Self-employed people, be they artists or artisans, have no long-term contracts to keep them alive. Instead, they rely on their skill and expertise, for a marketable skill is the ultimate security of a flexilife existence. But to be marketable, a skill needs to be certified, at least in the early years of practice. In time, the work done is its own diploma, but no one will ask you to do the first lot of work without some assurance that you can do it. A name on a business card with "plumber" or "publicity" underneath it is no guarantee in itself that the bearer can either plumb or publicize. Credentials, in other words, will be an essential but, alas, not a sufficient starting point.

Credentials may guarantee you the chance of work and money in a Dionysian society, but if work or, at any rate, paid work is no longer the whole of life for all of life, if there will be big chunks of time during or after one's working life that will be for other things, then credentials alone will not define you or your success. They will, however, free you to be more than your official work, more than your credentials.

Replacing the employment society with the credential society may therefore allow society to develop many more models and definitions of success, the good life, and fulfillment. A full-employment society divided life into the job—and leisure. Success was conventionally defined as success in the job, although many always knew, and others often found, that it was things outside the job that mattered most: the family, the garden, sports, or the community. The employment society is by its nature materialist and careerist, because those are its motivating weapons. If no one needed money or career advancement, Apollonian structures would lose their grip. A more Dionysian society will have plenty of materialists, no doubt, and we should be grateful for that, for we need their wealth-creating drive, but there must also be other models to choose from. Quality in life is not totally dependent on quantity, and some will use their new

freedom and their new discretionary time to develop new interests, travel more, lead a simpler life, invest in their families, put a
toe into local politics, get involved in voluntary work, or just read
more, watch more television, or talk with friends. Success will
have, I hope, many faces, of which the careerist professional will
be only one.

For some, this freeing up of pathways will be confusing.
Choice is often more worrying than no choice. The point of life
will be less obvious if money is no longer the main criterion. How
will we judge people? How will we judge ourselves? How will we
know whether our prospective son- or daughter-in-law has good
prospects when "prospects" can be so widely defined? The new
paradigm offers a cafeteria of possibilities for life; it is an opportunity to choose one's own set of credentials and a lifestyle to fit.
It will lead to an interesting and varied society, but also one that
will be confusing to many, particularly to those who are not
naturally Dionysian or who do not find credentials easy to come
by and have valued the routine and the security of employment.
Sadly, the professionalization of the Apollonian cultures that remain will mean that those who are least able to cope with life
beyond employment will be among the first to be pushed into it.
The credential society will not be everyone's dream and might
well be the basis for a new class division between those with
credentials and those without them.

The New Questions

The exciting possibilities of new patterns of organizations, jobs,
and life should not blind us to the problems and, in particular, to
the three key questions:

- What are we going to live on?
- How are we going to educate ourselves?
- How can we protect ourselves?

These are the enabling questions of the new scenario. If we
can't answer them correctly, we shall divide society into those
who can work, have jobs, and make money and those who cannot. It will be a society of escalating envy and resentment, in

which those who make money will resent paying high taxes to keep alive those who don't or can't work, and they in turn will resent their dependency and envy the privileges and the lifestyle of those in jobs.

Money and education are the pathways to freedom. Without them, a person is trapped, physically and psychologically. It is no use advising people to "get on their bikes" and look for work, as one employment minister did in Britain, if they don't have bikes, let alone cars, in the first place (and at that date less than 10 percent of Britain's unemployed did own a bike); if they can't sell their houses or find another one on oversubscribed housing lists; or if they don't have the skills required in the new jobs. Money and education are the most sensible investments that any society can make in its citizens, particularly the less fortunate ones, but they have to be seen as an investment, not a grudging handout. If the investment is not made, we might well be heading for a Gor-Saga society. It is an investment, however, about which we cannot wait for society as a whole to make up its mind: Organizations themselves need to take a lead if they want to end up in a world worth living in.

The Gor-Saga Society

In her novel *Gor-Saga,* Maureen Duffy describes, as a background to the plot, a world in which the meritocracy, in their professional jobs, has taken over.[6] Control of the technology gives to the officials of organizations control of information and the power to run people's lives and even, maybe, to create life of the sort they want.

Excluded from this society are the "nons," those without proper jobs, who live in encampments on the edges of cities or deep in the country. Violence is rife and even volunteer agencies have had to become armed guerrillas in order to be effective. The cities have become ghettos for the rich and for tourists, and passes are needed for the best suburbs.

There are trains and buses and television and all the paraphernalia of life, but it is a proper life only for the credentialed few and a jungle existence for the many, a world in which *word processor* has become a polite term for a machine minder and *pensioner* means anyone, of any age, who cannot provide for himself or herself.

What Are We Going to Live On?

Put rather starkly, if we are working half the hours we used to and if we can look forward to twice as many years after employment, we should be putting aside, as a nation or as individuals, four times as much money for our retirement. Nothing like that is happening, although it could be argued that in Britain at least, people have been overinvesting in their pensions for years, because it was so tax effective to do so, and have therefore been unwittingly preparing for the kind of future that is in store.

That would be true if everyone had been doing it and if pensions were universally regarded as an individual's accumulating capital rather than his right to a wage or salary after he has left employment. As it is, early leavers or frequent movers lose most of the organization's contributions and fund the fuller pensions of those who stay. Organizations and their pension funds must recognize the realities of modern organizational life, of truncated careers and flexilives, if they want to make it easier for people to move out, to subcontract, or to work part time.

Dionysians have individual pension plans, and so-called portable pensions will surely become more common as Dionysians become more fashionable in and around organizations. But portable and personal pension schemes are inevitably more expensive, or put it the other way round, they produce lower pensions because they cannot take so much actuarial account of all those early leavers and frequent movers. In the new scenario, therefore, most of us will be poorer than we would have been, unless we do something.

This "something" must start with increased contributions, by both organization and individual, but these will not be forthcoming unless and until people really understand that careers will be shorter and life after employment longer. It is critical to their own futures that managers and employees understand how organizations are changing. Making last-minute provision, as happens today when top executives retire early, will be ruinously expensive when it happens on a larger scale. Making no last-minute provision, on the other hand, can condemn a loyal colleague to poverty, for it is unrealistic to expect the state to find the funds to make up the difference. Brave talk of reducing the official retirement age always peters out when the cost is calculated. In the end, a large part of an individual's later-life money has to come from midlife savings.

Savings—or deferred pay if you like to see it that way—will never, however, be enough for most. Many will want and need to top it off with some marginal work, often at low or marginal wages. Fortunately, the more Dionysian nature of work will make this possible for anyone with a marketable skill or talent and the energy and zeal to sell it. People will be pushed toward part-time self-employment because they will still be young enough to work and to want the rewards. For some, however, it will not be making money but saving money that will be important—doing things for themselves instead of paying others to do them. Self-sufficiency is a form of domestic import substitution and is just as effective as increasing exports. But self-sufficiency is only another form of self-employment, except that it is done for oneself, not for others.

The central message is clear: Necessity will make Dionysians of us all, later if not sooner. Individuals must adjust to this—and organizations would be sensible to help them in that adjustment, particularly by making better financial provision for their life beyond employment—because no state will be able to afford to do it adequately.

The state, however, could usefully start to regard unemployment benefits, supplementary benefits, and pensions as basic incomes, and not as alternatives to income. Then, any earnings over and above these basics would not be penalized so heavily. Current rules make entrepreneurship a crime for anyone out of work, when it should be the best possible medicine for them and for society. We need, in fact, to rethink our whole approach to welfare now that full-time jobs are the prerequisite of only half the adult working population. We could make a start by banning the word *unemployment* and talking of *temporarily self-employed*, like actors or writers, of people who need to supplement their income but are still in the working population, and of Dionysians, not failed Apollonians.

How Are We Going to Educate Ourselves?

Money, however, as it is so often, is only part of the problem, even if it is the part that hurts, the presenting problem. If a Dionysian life is, at some stage or other, to be forced on all of us, we shall have to learn new skills, new habits, and new attitudes.

Schools have long been Apollonian organizations, educating people for Apollonian lives in formal organizations. As we have seen, there are signs that schools, like other organizations, will change into something more like networks, with more Athenian and Dionysian characteristics, but the change won't be in time to affect or interest any of those likely to read this book. For them, the institutions of education will have to be the work organization, with help whenever possible from the further and higher education system.

The first requirement, after all, of a Dionysian life is a marketable skill or talent. Examination results, a career of ever more important management jobs, and a record of international or industrial experience are of little use unless they can be turned into a product that someone wants. In self-employment, unlike employment, it is not the person that people are interested in, but the product that he or she is offering. Professionals, therefore, have it easy, because their qualification is, in effect, a license to sell their skill. Professionals can be Dionysians outside or inside the organization, and it is easier for them to move away and practice on their own account than it is for someone whose main job has been to coordinate and manage. What does a manager do without people to manage?

The De-skilled Executive

The account executive was depressed. He had just been laid off from his advertising firm, at the age of forty-eight. He was anxious to find another job, but at his age there were few openings in the advertising world.

"What are you good at?" I asked.

"Running an account group in an advertising agency," he replied.

"Well, that won't get you very far."

"I know, but that's all I'm any good at."

I suggested that he ask twenty friends or associates

over the next two weeks to tell him one thing he was good at. Two weeks later, he came back with a list of twenty talents. He was excited but puzzled. "Not one of them mentioned running an account group!"

Working on and developing his unsuspected talents opened up new avenues and new kinds of work. Organizations can keep bits of you hidden from yourself.

More people need more opportunities to discover talents and abilities that they can turn into products and useful work. "Continuing education" needs to become more of a reality and not just a way of learning a new hobby or improving one's holidays with better language skills and a knowledge of history. Pre-retirement education should be about the development of skills and the capacity for self-employment, rather than lectures about keeping fit and maintaining the home.

In time, maybe, governments will pick up the idea of educational credits for people in midlife, to be cashed in at the institution of one's choice at a time of one's choice. In time, more schools will make their skills available to all in the community and not just to the kids. In time, it will become easier and more respectable for people over forty to study part time for a degree and to take time off work to study. Organizations, however, would be wise not to wait for governments but to make it their responsibility to see that individuals equip themselves for life beyond employment while they are still employed. It is, after all, as important to equip someone to earn money as it is to give them money—and it might be cheaper.

Asking organizations to equip someone to be independent sounds like asking them to plot their own downfall. But good Dionysian organizations know that their strength lies in their best people, despite the risk that those people are always the ones who would find it easiest to leave. Keeping people dependent has never worked, in families or organizations. Organizations need therefore to think of themselves as schools, although schools of a very different sort, places where people can acquire, develop, and practice skills that will be useful all their lives. And they need to encourage people to acquire relevant qualifications that will be their passport to self-employment at some stage.

They need, in other words, to encourage people to acquire the means to freedom, even if they sometimes set themselves free before the organization would have wanted it. Better that than a group of dependants growing older and more scared of the world outside.

How Will We Project Ourselves?

Money and education are the pathways to self-employment, but it remains an insecure and ill-protected way of life for most. They may have a skill, a willingness to work, aptitude, and talent, but selling themselves is another matter. The self-employed home worker has traditionally been the most exploited of all workers, and there is little sign that this has improved much, although the technology has changed from the loom to the computer terminal.

The traditional professions have their associations, which are supposed to maintain standards as well as to seek fair rewards. Some self-employed have agents who sell and negotiate on behalf of their artists or their actors or their writers. Some form cooperatives to share facilities or to promote their wares. Others join networks, loose associations, which print lots of names, convene conferences, publish newsletters, and generally provide a way of keeping in touch.

We shall need to see more of each. In a sense, the guilds need to be recreated, both to set standards and to look after the interests of their members, because those potential members will be up against strong forces. Their markets will, in many cases, be organizations, not people, and organizations can deal roughly with people smaller than themselves, paying them late, bargaining down the rate of pay, keeping contracts short, and insisting on unreasonable delivery arrangements. Not all organizations will act responsibly.

The role of the unions is critical to all of this. The unions emerged as the protector of the employee. Will they continue to interpret this as meaning the protection of the individual *only* as an employee, or will they broaden their scope to include the individual in any relationship with the organization? It is in their own interest to broaden their mandate, for the decline of employment will otherwise inevitably mean the decline of unions as their membership continues to dwindle. Employment à la carte is the message of the future. If the unions stick to only one dish, they will effectively signal their own demise.

Change or Decay?

Many organizations do not change; they only fade away, and others spring up to take their place. Unable to contemplate a future different from all that they have been used to, they continue to beaver away at what they know best how to do, working harder and more efficiently on a diminishing task. Education, for instance, is the growth sector of every society, yet everywhere the formal education system is contracting or closing, and the educational profession is in recession and retreat. Meanwhile, computer manufacturers, book publishers, video filmmakers, language schools, and summer camps are booming. Education, yes, but not in schools, it seems. Indeed, as educational networks become more common and more available, we may see the school dropout age lowered, leaving people, perhaps financed by vouchers, to choose their own sources of learning while schools contract even more.

Unions may be turning their backs on the future, but they are only copying firms who are reluctant to change their patterns of employment, their promises of careers for all, or their assumptions that the place can function only if everyone is at work all the time.

Unusually, however, and fortunately, their destiny is in their own hands. Organizations may wither and decay instead of changing, but it does not have to be that way. This book is written in the hope that if more managers understand what is happening and what possibilities are open to them, then more will experiment with the future instead of ignoring it. Change, after all, in the American tradition, does not come about as a result of edicts from the center but because of new case law, which after a time becomes established practice, incorporated in the law of the land. It is more experiments we need, to change organizational fashion, even if some, as is their wont, are not successful. Without them, our society may well decay as its organizations wither.

NOTES AND REFERENCES

Chapter 1

1. M. Maccoby, *The Gamesman: The New Corporate Leaders* (London: Secker & Warburg, 1978).

Chapter 2

1. Described in his book *The Nature of Managerial Work* (New York: Harper & Row, 1973).

2. H. Mintzberg, "Planning on the Left Side, Managing on the Right," *Harvard Business Review*, July–August 1976.

3. L. Klein, *New Forms of Work Organisation* (Cambridge: Cambridge University Press, 1976).

4. See E. Jacques, *A General Theory of Bureaucracy* (London: Heinemann, 1976).

5. The questionnaire is adapted from one originally developed by Dr. Roger Harrison.

Chapter 3

1. Based on B. P. Indik, "Some Effects of Organisation Size on Member Attitudes and Behaviour," *Human Relations* 16 (1963): 369–84.

2. H. J. Eysenck and G. Wilson, *Know Your Own Personality* (London: Pelican, 1976).

3. See R. Stewart, *Contrasts in Management* (New York: McGraw-Hill, 1976).

4. P. R. Lawrence and J. W. Lorsc, *Organisation and Environment* (Cambridge, MA: Harvard University Press, 1967).

Chapter 4

1. G. Hofstede, *Culture's Consequences—International Differences in Work-Related Values* (London, 1980).

2. G. Hofstede, "Managing Differences in the Multicultural Organization," *Organizational Dynamics,* Summer 1980.

3. W. Ouchi, *Theory Z* (Reading, MA: Addison-Wesley, 1981).

4. R. Pascale and A. G. Athos, *The Art of Japanese Management* (London: Penguin, 1981).

5. S. Kamate, *Japan in the Passing Crowd* (London: Allen & Unwin, 1983).

6. Ouchi, *Theory Z.*

7. T. H. Peters and R. Waterman Jr., *In Search of Excellence* (New York: Harper & Row, 1982).

8. R. M. Kanter, *The Change Masters* (London: Allen & Unwin, 1983).

Chapter 5

1. Of course, pure capitalist theory would have all surplus earnings returned to the owners, who would then decide where it was appropriate to reinvest them. But this "city-state" view of the capitalist notion implies a more perfect market, better information, and speedier decision processes than could in practice exist, so the managerial prerogative has become enlarged until managers have acquired the right to reinvest their earnings in the continuation of the business. Due payment must be made, in dividends or interest, for the use of the capital, but the capital itself is seldom returned voluntarily to the owners.

2. S. J. Prais, *The Evolution of Giant Firms in Britain* (Cambridge: Cambridge University Press, 1977).

3. L. Hannah and J. Kay, *Concentration in Modern Industry* (London: Macmillan, 1977).

4. In his stimulating booklet "Beyond Bureaucracy," 1976, available from Management Research.

5. See D. T. N. Williamson, "The Anachronistic Factory," *Personnel Review,* Autumn 1973.

6. R. M. Kanter, *The Change Managers: Corporate Entrepreneurs at Work* (London: Allen & Unwin, 1983).

7. D. Yankelovitch Inc., *The Changing Values on Campus* (New York: Washington Square Press, 1972).

8. M. Olson, *The Rise and Decline of Nations* (New Haven, CT: Yale University Press, 1982).

9. J. H. Dunning, "U.S. Subsidiaries in Britain and Their U.K. Competitors," *Business Ratios,* June 1968, p. 16.

10. C. Handy et al., *The Making of Managers* (London: NEDO 1988).

11. N. Morse and R. Weiss, "The Function and Meaning of Work and Job," *American Sociological Review* (1955).

12. H. Hansen, *The British Manager* (Cambridge, MA: Harvard University Press, 1976).

13. From *Essays in Persuasion* (New York: Norton Library, 1963), and quoted by Gurth Higgin in his inaugural address (1975) at Loughborough University of Technology, entitled "Scarcity, Abundance and Depletion."

Chapter 6

1. M. Wiener, *English Culture and the Decline of the Industrial Spirit, 1850–1890* (Cambridge: Cambridge University Press, 1981).

2. Reported in *The Sunday Times* (London), 6 March 1977.

3. F. K. Foulkes and A. Whitman, "Full Employment, Product/ Marketing Strategies," Human Resources Policy Institute, Boston University, 1984.

4. E. Johns, "Where Smallness Pays," *Management Today,* July 1976.

5. D. T. N. Williamson, "The Anachronistic Factory," *Personnel Review,* Autumn 1973.

Chapter 7

1. A. Toffler, *Future Shock* (London: Pan 1971).

2. H. Mintzberg, *Structure in Firms* (Englewood Cliffs, NJ: Prentice-Hall, 1983).

3. N. Foy, *The Yin and Yang of Organisations* (London: Grant McIntyre, 1981).

4. N. Macrae, "Intrapreneurial Now," *The Economist,* 17 April 1982.

5. See D. Sheane, *Beyond Bureaucracy* (London: Management Research, 1976).

6. Reported by Colin Ward in *Anarchy in Action* (London: Allen & Unwin, 1973).

Chapter 8

1. G. Rattray Taylor, *How to Avoid the Future* (London: New English Library, 1978).

2. Reported in *The Economist,* 19 May 1984.

3. R. Rose, *Getting by in Three Economies* (London: Centre for Study of Public Policy, 1983).

4. As reported by J. Thornley in *Worker's Co-operatives* (London: Heinemann, 1981).

5. Reported by Opinion Research and Communication, "Worker Aspirations and Revised EEC Proposals on Worker Involvement" 1983.

6. (London: Methuen, 1981).

INDEX